More Little Known Tales in California History

Alton Pryor

More Little Known Tales in California History

Alton Pryor

Stagecoach Publishing
5360 Campcreek Loop
Roseville, CA 95747
916-771-8166

More Little Known Tales in California History

Library of Congress Control Number 2007904754

ISBN: 9780966005301

Stagecoach Publishing
5360 Campcreek Loop
Roseville, CA. 95747
Email: stagecoach@surewest.net
916-771-8166

History is indeed little more than the register of the crimes, follies and misfortunes of mankind.

Edward Gibbon (1737-1794)

Table of Contents

Chapter 1
The Old Ridge Route   11

Chapter 2
The Old Plank Road   17

Chapter 3
Downfall of the Indians   25

Chapter 4
A Mexican Standoff   31

Chapter 5
California's Own Navy   37

Chapter 6
A Hunting Mishap   45

Chapter7
A City Built by A King   49

Chapter 8
Alcatraz   55

Chapter 9
The Vision of Ole Hanson   61

Chapter 10
The Sagebrush War   69

Chapter 11
    He Kept the Bank Open   75

Chapter 12
    A River with A Cause   81

Chapter 13
    He Left Civilization Behind   87

Chapter 14
    Indian Pollution Found   95

Chapter 15
    The Modoc Indian War   101

Chapter 16
    Girl Was Stolen by Indians   109

Chapter 17
    Gold in Southern California   115

Chapter 18
    St. George's Reef Light   119

Chapter 19
    California's State Flower   123

Chapter 20
    He Founded San Francisco   127

Chapter 21
    Dam Collapse Kills 500   131

Chapter 22
The Chinese Exclusion Act   137

Chapter 23
Big 'Blowup' in Roseville   145

Chapter 24
Crazy Stoddard's Lost Lake of Gold   153

Chapter 25
The Lost Cement Mines   163

Chapter 26
The Sea Otter Hunters   169

About the Author   180

Chapter 1

The Old Ridge Route

It isn't known whether the people in this early auto were sightseers or on the verge of going off the old Ridge Route.

When motorists traveled between Los Angeles and the San Joaquin Valley in 1915, they navigated 48 miles of tortuous hairpin turns and steep grades. This was famously known as the *Old Ridge Route*.

Because of the high number of vehicles using it, speed limits on the Old Ridge Route were 15 miles per hour for cars and 12 miles per hour for trucks. The 48-mile trip took the entire day.

The Old Ridge Route was one of the first projects of the newly formed California Highway Commission and was considered a "superhighway" during its day.

The old Ridge Route opened in 1915 and wasn't completely paved until 1919. It was still an improvement for travelers who would otherwise make the long trip around the mountains.

When it first opened in 1915, it was a graded dirt road with an oil surface. It was soon paved with a single slab of concrete.

The Old Ridge Route was the first highway built to cross the mountains directly. Before its construction, travelers either went by Highway 101 along the coast or ventured by way of Mojave and through the desert.

In construction the Ridge Route, mules were used to pull Fresno scrapers, a primitive device used to grade and construct roads.

The Tumble Inn was one of the roadside services on the Old Ridge Route.

When it opened in 1915, the route was lauded as the most scientifically constructed mountain road in the world. While it went over the steep mountains, grades did not exceed six or seven percent.

The road essentially united California, making travel between Los Angeles and the Central Valley possible in one day. Some historians contend that this link between southern and central California may have saved California from being split into two states.

Roadside services once dotted the Old Ridge Route. Gas stations, hotels, campsites, and restaurants, now long forgotten, were available. Some of these are now memorialized with roadside markers.

The Original Ridge Route starts at Castaic and winds its way over some 26 miles up to its highest point at 4,233 feet. It then descends to today's Highway 138 at Gorman.

These steps are all that remains of the old Tumble Inn.

Less than 20 years later, the original Ridge Route proved inadequate for the volume of traffic using it. It also became a very dangerous road, especially the Grapevine Grade section where autos suffered a very high accident rate in navigating its many sharp curves.

The old Ridge Route had a notorious accident rate.

The Old Ridge Route lost its allure when the *Ridge Route Alternative* (now Highway 99) was completed in 1933. This three-lane highway was more direct and soon grew to a four-lane highway.

Even this route became overcrowded. In 1926, Highway 99 was designated as an official U. S. Route.

Plans were made in 1940 to convert US 99 into a four-lane expressway, but World War II delayed any further widening work.

During the period of 1960 to 1967, I-5 replaced all of US 99. The building of I-5 through the Tehachapi's proved one of the most impressive public works projects in the highway system.

More dirt was used to grade for I-5 than was used to build the entire Aswan Dam in Egypt.

Chapter 2

The Old Plank Road

The Imperial Sand Dunes are the largest mass of sand dunes in California. This dune system extends for more than forty miles along the eastern edge of the Imperial Valley.

(Bureau of Land Management)

Automobiles were young, but far-sighted planners knew roads linking towns and communities would bring immense benefits.

Colonel Ed Fletcher, of San Diego, sponsored a road race to determine the best route between southern California and Phoenix,. In response, the Los Angeles Examiner issued a challenge to Fletcher. A reporter on the Examiner would compete with Fletcher to select the fastest route.

The race was set for October 12, when the temperatures in the normally blistering Imperial Desert cooled to balmy degrees. The reporter from the Examiner received a twenty-four hour head start, and his goal was to travel from Los Angeles to Phoenix by the quickest route he could devise.

Fletcher, traveling from San Diego to Phoenix, selected a route across the Imperial Sand Dunes, notorious for their ever-shifting sands that could mire the thin tires of the new automobiles.

The sly Fletcher perceived the danger in crossing the sandy terrain. He stationed a team of six horses at the dunes to pull his automobile through the heavy sand.

Fletcher won the race by making the trip in nineteen and one-half hours. It was thus determined that the Imperial Sand Hills Route was the best means of bringing automobile traffic across the desert.

It was Imperial County Supervisor Ed Boyd who conceived the idea to build a plank road across the dunes. The idea received a boost when the federal government and the states of California and Arizona announced that a bridge would be built across the Colorado River at Yuma, giving automobiles an easy river crossing.

The Plank Road became operational on April 4, 1915. (Bureau of Land Management)

To add even more feasibility to the plan, San Diego announced that it planned to hold an exhibition celebrating the opening of the Panama Canal in 1915. The event would lure thousands of visitors to San Diego, many traveling by automobile.

The next step was finding a reliable way to tame the shifting sand dunes and allow autos to travel across them.

One of the first plans called for laying a thick mat of arrow weed over the sand for autos to roll over. This plan worked until the weeds dried and became brittle. They then broke up and caused more of a problem than in the beginning.

Edward Johnson, a mechanic in Holtville, conceived another plan. He modified a Model T Ford by raising the drive shaft up under the seat and put enlarged tires on the rear wheels. When he headed for the dunes, he stalled going up the first sand hill, and the six men and horses that were with him had to pull him out.

When Supervisor Boyd proposed building a plank road, the idea was tested and won over other methods.

Construction of the first plank road began September 19, 1912. It was completed three weeks later. This first road was built entirely with free labor donated by the farmers of the Imperial Valley.

The travelers on the road also maintained it. When a person passed a damaged area, he would stop and fix it so that it would be passable on his return. This first road was only one lane wide and covered a distance of six miles over the worst of the sand dunes.

Fletcher raised the money to buy and ship 13,000 planks from San Diego to Holtville, just west of the dreaded sand dunes.

The Imperial County Board of Supervisors sweetened the pot with an $8,600 contribution.

L.F. "Newt" Gray was chosen to supervise construction of the plank road. He first drilled a well on the western edge of the Sand Hills and found water. This spot became well known as "Gray's Well, and served as a work camp for the construction crew.

Even though turnouts were installed every one-fourth mile along the old plank road, fistfights often erupted between travelers who claimed right of way. (Cal Trans Photo)

There was great fanfare when the first planks were laid on February 14, 1915. During the next two months, a combination of paid workers and volunteers hauled lumber and laid down two parallel plank tracks.

Each track was twenty-five feet wide. The planks were spiked to wooden cross bars underneath. This plank road floated across six-and-one-half miles of shifting sand east of Gray's Well.

The workers finished the wooden roadway on April 4, 1915. A week later, twenty-five cars carrying more than one hundred passengers, traveled over the plank road.

For most of its length, the Plank Road was an eight-foot wide wooden driveway. Because it was a single lane road, turnouts were constructed every one-fourth mile to allow passage of vehicles going in opposite directions.

Even then there was road rage. Fistfights often broke out when one vehicle or another would not yield the right of way on the narrow road.

Building a road on the shifting sand dunes is considered a marvelous feat. The sand hills themselves are actually a sea of rounded particles of sand and range up to seven miles wide and more than fifty feet long.

The dunes drift with the wind and never stay in one place. Some parts move at a slow rate of only a few feet per day. But there are some dunes that can move up to 50 feet per hour.

Ed Fletcher, who promoted the plank road across the dunes, later rose to prominence as Director of California Department of Public Works.

The first version of the plank road lasted only one year. The completion of the "Ocean to Ocean Highway Bridge" in 1915, crossing the Colorado River at Yuma, Arizona increased traffic on the road, necessitating construction of a new version.

The second version of the road was built in eight foot by twelve-foot sections at a plant at Ogilby, a small town ten miles east of the road. The completed sections were stacked and ready to install when they were hauled to the road site.

A tongue and groove design fitted the sections into each other, keeping them in place on the shifting sand.

In 1927, the state constructed a two-lane asphalt road from Holtville to Yuma. This stretch of highway was completed a year later. Instead of shovels manned by men, snowplows were used to clear the sand from the highway.

From 1915 to 1919, travel between Yuma and Holtville could be accomplished in three or four hours. When traffic increased from 1919 to 1927, the trip became much longer.

Fights between drivers over right-of-way caused traffic jams of eight to ten cars that could not move until the antagonists settled their argument. It often took hours to back the jammed cars to a turnout so other cars could pass. Trips then took as long as two days. Many travelers camped in the middle of the sand dunes.

Travelers carried extra equipment when traversing the dunes. This included extra boards, two auto jacks, gunnysacks, a shovel, and food and water for at least two days.

A warning in the *Imperial Valley Post Press* on Sunday, April 29, 1919, gave travelers second thoughts.

"Warning. Avoid the plank road. A public warning was issued yesterday by the El Centro branch of the auto club of southern California that travel to Yuma via the plank road is dangerous. Several cars which attempted the trip were badly damaged and owners were put to heavy expense to get through. Cars are injured in the drive gears, engines are sacked and shattered, and in many cases the machines have to be pulled many miles by teams. Parties attempting to travel suffer from thirst and hunger and are sometimes in danger of death as there is little chance of succor arriving unless a call for aid reaches Holtville or Yuma."

First Plank Roads

The original idea for wood plank roads came from Russia to Canada in the 1830's and became, for a short time, a popular method of construction. The idea spread to the U.S. in the 1840's.

Some of the roads disappeared, others are now just trails, many became paved roads, but in many cases the name stuck and you can still find signs that the road was once a "Plank Road.

Chapter 3

'Downfall' of the Indians

This early painting shows Indians and government
officials negotiating terms of a treaty.

J uan Rodriguez Cabrillo, in 1542, claimed
Alta California for the Spanish crown.
Thirty-seven years later, Francis Drake
explored what is now California's coast.

Junipero Serra, founder of California mission system.

The visiting Europeans are known to have carried diseases to Latin America that were unknown to the region. Historians now believed that European sailors left the seeds of their various diseases with the natives of California.

Some say it was the building of the Spanish missions in 1769 along the California coast that started many problems among the Alta California Indians.

Dr. Edward Castillo is a professor of *Native American Studies* at Sonoma State University. He is Cahuilla and Luiseño Indian himself. He is harsh in his assessment of what happened to Native Americans when the Spanish established their mission system.

From the native viewpoint the Spanish invasion and occupation was a catastrophe of indescribable proportions...Hispanos first infected the neophytes with venereal disease, which quickly spread to non-mission tribes as early as 1800 and thereafter increased steadily.

Historians face a problem in dealing with the injustice to Native Americans because there is a lack of accurate information. Indians have left no written records of their views, making it a difficult situation to analyze without bias.

"One fact that has become clear through recent mission studies is that Indian peoples were not simply passive recipients of European culture," say Castillo and his colleague Robert H. Jackson.

More than one reviewer of the writings of Castillo and Jackson take issue with the historians. Jack S. Williams, Center for Spanish Colonial Archaeology and Anita Cohen-Williams, are two such dissenters.

They say Castillo and Jackson take delight in attacking Junipero Serra, the founder of the California Mission system.

The discovery of gold at Sutter's Mill added another dimension to the treatment of Native Californios. Tribes came into full contact with the gold seekers. The Indians had no use for gold, but they were aware of its existence.

While the padres were sincere and enthusiastic in their desire to preach the gospel, the soldiers who accompanied them were not. The soldiers were recruited from the lowest ranks of Spanish society.

The soldiers pursued the Indian women, causing conflict with Indian tribes. This led to the presidios and the missions being established at some distance from one another. Later, it was advocated that only married soldiers be recruited, and that they bring their wives with them to the new country.

California Indians were often taken advantage of by gold rush storekeepers. (

Natives, who often knew where gold could be found, sometimes led prospectors to rich diggings. Storekeepers and other tradesmen often took advantage of local Indians in the trading of goods.

They traded cheap glass beads to the Indians for an equal weight in gold. One storekeeper did the same with an Indian who wanted to purchase raisins. The Indian placed a rag containing gold flakes on one side of the balancing scale. Onto the other side, the storekeeper carefully counted out raisins, one at a time, until their weight balanced that of the gold. Both the Indian and the storekeeper were happy.

A California artist portrays a priest and an Indian.

Gold miners sometimes changed the face of the land on which the Indians depended so much for their livelihood. For example, mining refuse clogged the Yuba River with so much mud and debris that it raised the level of the river more than thirty feet.

The City of Marysville found itself beneath the surface of the rivers' water. The city then depended on sometimes hastily thrown up levees for protection.

There was an estimated one-hundred-thousand Indians in California. Some said California was crowded with more Indians per square mile than any other portion of the pre-European United States.

Most often, the Indians were hunters and gatherers. Early mission records show them to be a healthy people. The Indians lived in villages near streams, near the ocean, or near groves of live oaks.

Indian craftsmen made baskets so tightly wove they would hold water. The Indians, indeed, were a contented people. As such, they could see little reason to let the white padres convert them to strange languages and practices.

The missions were intended to be temporary. As soon as a mission's work was done in one area, it would move on to another. This worked in Peru, Central America and Mexico.

But in California, no ten-year mission was successful. When the order came through to secularize the missions after sixty-five years of operation, none of California's twenty-one missions was ready to be run by the Indians.

Chapter 4

A 'Mexican Standoff'

Did the U.S. Steal California?

Five hundred Mexican soldiers stood on the bluff overlooking the San Gabriel River. The month and day was January 8 and the year was 1842.

The sparse militia was the last of the Mexican military force available to resist the U.S. forces occupying *Alta California*.

The Mexicans faced 600 U.S. troops advancing from San Diego. General Stephen Watts Kearny and U.S. Navy Captain Robert F. Stockton led these troops.

When the troops reached the San Gabriel River, the Mexicans opened fire. Two hours of artillery duels, and several unsuccessful Mexican charges, followed.

General Jose Maria Flores, commander of the Mexicans, conceded the battle and withdrew. The Americans seized the bluff that was occupied by the Mexicans, along with abandoned Mexican artillery.

The following day, General Flores engaged the advancing Americans at the Battle of La Mesa (in modern-day Vernon). Although the Mexicans offered a more intense fight, and managed to envelop the American force, Flores soon realized he could not stop this advance and ordered a withdrawal.

When Mexican leaders in Los Angeles learned of the unsuccessful efforts by Flores and his militia, they gave up hope of a successful defense and surrendered the city peacefully to the American commanders.

General John Fremont

Flores learned that another daunting American force, led by Army Lieutenant Colonel John C. Fremont was marching from the north to meet up with Kearny and Stockton.

He realized the futility of his situation. Flores turned his command over to Andres Pico and fled to unoccupied Mexico. Pico was left with few options. He agreed to meet with Fremont to discuss terms of surrender.

Pico signed the *Treaty of Cahuenga* with Fremont, effectively surrendering all of *Alta California* to the United States.

The Mexican American War (1846-1848) was brief, but it's importance lies in the fact that it was instrumental in shaping the geographical boundaries of the United States.

There are many Chicano activists who contend that California was "stolen" from Mexico. Let's take a look backwards at history.

The annexation of Texas caused an immediate rupture between the United States and Mexico, which had never honored Texas' independence.

There was another serious dispute between the United States and Mexico. Mexico, which had been impoverished by its own civil war, did not hesitate to plunder American vessels in the Gulf of Mexico to replenish its treasury.

In 1831, a treaty was agreed to between the two nations that included redress for the robberies of its ships. These promises were never fulfilled, and worse, the robberies continued.

By 1840, Mexicans had appropriated more than six million dollars worth of property belonging to

Americans. The claim for this amount was still unsatisfied when the annexation of Texas took place.

Zachary Taylor's Army of Occupation in Mexico for the defense of Texas)

President James K. Polk ordered General Zachary Taylor, head of the United States troops in the Southwest, to go to Texas and position his men as close to the Rio Grande as prudence would allow.

The Mexicans were itching for war. A large force of Mexican soldiers attacked the American army in an attempt to drive them back from the Rio Grande. The Americans considered the Rio Grande as its border with Mexico.

General Zachary Taylor

President James K. Polk declared, "American blood has been shed on American soil." He asked Congress for a declaration of war.

War was declared on Mexico on May 13, 1846.

A treaty of peace was concluded between Mexico and the U.S., called The Treaty of Guadalupe-Hidalgo. Both governments on July 4, 1848 ratified it.

The treaty called for the evacuation of American troops from Mexico within three months. It also provided for the payment of three million dollars in hand, and twelve million dollars more in four annual installments by the U.S. to Mexico for the territories of New Mexico and California.

It should be pointed out that only about 80,000 Mexicans lived in the entire southwest. Mexico also exercised little control over the territory.

Michael Warder, a scholar at the Claremont Institute, wrote, "From 1821, the end of Spanish rule, through 1847, Mexico endured 50 military regimes, five constitutional conventions, and three constitutions." Mexico also suffered through 11 different terms of leadership under the tragic president and general, Antonio Lopez de Santa Anna.

Still, it's important to note that the immediate cause for the Mexican-American War was a $3 million debt to America for damages done by Mexicans to Americans. The Mexican government agreed to pay the bill, but was repeatedly in default.

President James Polk and others believed that if the United States didn't acquire California, Great Britain or other exploiters might. Despite winning the war, America paid $18 million for the territory., and lost 13,000 lives during the brief skirmish.

The Mexican-American War was the U.S. Army's first experience at waging an extended conflict in a foreign land. At the conclusion of the conflict, the U.S. added Texas, Arizona, New Mexico, and California to its holdings, as well as portions of Colorado, Wyoming, Utah and Nevada.

Chapter 5

California's Own Navy

California Naval Militia in formation at Santa Fe Depot.

(San Diego Historical Society)

In the late 1800s, California was virtually defenseless. There was little or no transit between the coasts of the U.S.

Even the U.S. naval force in the Pacific was insignificant, being composed of only sixty-four ships, and nearly one-third of them wooden at that. These ships dated from the Civil War or earlier, and were driven by steam or sail.

California's 1849 Constitution provided authority for the formation of both an "army and navy of this State." The formation of a naval militia was not possible until 1891, when California's legislature passed an act to establish a naval battalion. The battalion would be attached to the National Guard of California,

The USS Oregon (BB-3), of Spanish American War fame, was loaned to the State of California as a training ship for the Naval Battalion. (California State Military Archives)

The act provided for four companies of naval militia. When the first company of naval reserves was formed in August 1891, it made California one of the first of the Pacific States to muster a naval militia.

It wasn't long before California's Navy saw action. On April 1, 1898, the U.S. and Spain engaged in a war. The regiments and companies of the National Guard of California, including its navy battalion, were mobilized.

By 1899, California's Naval Battalion had grown to a total of 35 officers and 488 seamen. The United States considered California's naval militia as its reserve force.

While the U.S. Department of the Navy supplied the vessels and equipment used by California's navy, it had no control of the battalion.

This led the U.S. Secretary of the Navy to spearhead the move for establishment of a national naval militia, on the same lines of the land militia.

The act allowed any former enlisted man of the U.S. Navy or Marine Corps to enter the naval militia without professional examination, and at the same rate or rank he last held in the Navy or Marine Corps.

When the Naval Militia Act of February 16, 1914, was passed, it gave the U.S. Department of the Navy control of the naval militias of California and other states.

It was Captain George William Bauer that is credited with building the California Naval Militia Corps into a taut military organization. When he assumed charge of the militia in 1901, the service seemed hopelessly demoralized.

There were more discouragements than inducements for the young men to enlist as volunteer reservists. Such drills as were held were considered so elementary as to be of little practical value.

When Captain Bauer took command, the militia had five skeletal divisions that included two hundred fifty officers and men. Captain Bauer built this branch into such a popular service that it grew to nine strong divisions with a total enrollment of seven hundred volunteer blue jackets and their officers.

Bauer pressed the legislature to make more liberal allowances for the Naval Militia. He requisitioned the federal government for better equipment and succeeded in securing the latest model small arms, gatlings and rapid-fire guns, cutters and small-boats, along with the full use of several gunboats as training vessels.

The gunboat Marion was placed at the disposal of the Naval Militia, replacing the Comanche, a relic of the Civil War, which was never put to sea. Bauer next secured the USS Alert as the training ship for his state naval forces.

Four years later, the cruiser Marblehead was added as the flagship of the little navy.

Bauer realized that to attract the right kind of recruits, special inducements had to be offered. He inaugurated a series of practice cruises that afforded the men wholesome outdoor sport as well as highly instructive practice.

Under his command, Bauer's little navy did indeed become a disciplined functioning unit. In 1912, in the Straits of Juan de Fuca, the gunners of the Marblehead established the world's record for accuracy with the 4-inch rifle.

This was accomplished despite the fact that the ammunition and gun-sights were said to be in miserable condition.

Navy Goes Airborne

Eugene Ely sits at controls of his Curtiss biplane when he landed on the deck of a cruiser.
(Naval Historical Center)

It was a member of the National Guard that took the navy to the air. That man was Eugene Burton Ely.

Naval officials were taking notice of the airplane and the possibilities of adapting it to the navy's operations.

Ely, who learned of the navy's interest in flying an airplane to and from a ship, volunteered for the task. The plane was placed on board the scout cruiser *Birmingham* on which a platform had been built on the ship's foredeck. The structure sloped down five degrees from the cruiser's bridge to her bow to provide a gravity-assisted fifty-seven-foot takeoff run for Ely's Curtiss pusher airplane.

Dreadful weather and rainsqualls kept delaying the scheduled flight plan. Ely waited with anxious officials, hoping the weather would clear. As more clouds moved in, Ely soon concluded that if he were to make the test flight, he must do so immediately.

Ely gunned the engine of the Curtiss biplane, gave the release signal to the crew, and rolled down the ramp. The Curtiss touched the water, throwing ocean spray up with enough force to damage the propeller. The intense vibration of the plane warned Ely, a non-swimmer, that a quick landing was essential.

After some five minutes in the air, Ely touched down on Willoughby Spit. Even though the flight was considered more of a stunt than a test flight, it did receive wide publicity, exciting the public and the navy about the possibilities.

Another flight plan was hatched to overcome the weather-plagued disaster with the *Birmingham.* On this one, Eugene Ely would land and take off from the armored cruiser *Pennsylvania, but this time,* across the country in San Francisco Bay.

Ely and his helpers devised a way to stop the plane on the 120 by 30 foot deck. They stretched rope lines, attached to sand bags, across the deck. The ropes were raised high enough to catch the hooks attached to the airplane's landing gear.

As an emergency measure, in case the plane should overrun or swerve off the platform's edge, the crew rigged canvas awnings in front and to the sides.

Eugene Ely takes off from the cruiser *Pennsylvania* in San Francisco Bay, marking the first time an aviator had landed and taken off from a ship.
(Naval Historical Center)

The takeoff moment arrived. Just before 11 a.m., 18 January 1911 Ely flew from Tanforan racetrack to the waiting Pennsylvania.

In the bay, just off San Francisco's waterfront, the *Pennsylvania* rode to the flood tide, a breeze of 10 to 15 mph on her starboard quarter. Fifteen minutes after takeoff, Ely's plane was sighted one-half mile from the *Pennsylvania's* bridge.

Ely kept dropping his plane until it was still at a height of 100 feet while only 500 yards from the *Pennsylvania's* starboard quarter.

As Ely guided the plane to the platform, an unexpected updraft struck the aircraft. Ely was quick to respond. He dove the aircraft so that it snagged the arresting lines. The Curtiss was pulled to a smooth stop before reaching any of the safety barriers.

After a celebratory lunch with his wife and the *Pennsylvania's* Commanding Officer, Captain Charles F. Pond, Ely returned to the task of taking off from the deck of the ship.

Remounting his airplane, Ely made history again by being the first aviator to take off from the deck of a naval vessel.

The Navy began the slow process of bringing flying machines into its operations. It was the British Royal Navy, however that would take the lead in developing aircraft-carrying warships.

Chapter 6

A Hunting Mishap

(This story has been passed down through three generations. Some say it was true, while others pass it off as a practical joke that took on a life of its own. Verification has been difficult if not impossible, but it is such a good story, that we want to pass it on.

W.S. Cornelius, who came to California in 1882 when he was 20-years old, told the story to his children and grandchildren. Cornelius got a job driving jerk-line mule teams from Marysville and Willows up to the gold mines.

On his way back from the mines, he would stop and shoot game to sell in the Sacramento Valley. Deer would sell for fifty cents to a dollar each, a good price at the time.

Cornelius knew of a certain spot on the Feather River where the deer migrated down from the mountains when the snow season began. The young deer merchant would sit in a chair on the edge of a clearing when the fall deer migration began.

The cold air coming down the hill would carry Cornelius' scent away from the deer.

He shot the youngest and fattest of the migrating deer and stored them in a nearby ice cave until he had a wagonload. Unlike trophy hunters,

Cornelius shied from shooting the big bucks with the giant antlers. They were too tough when cooked. He considered killing these animals as "trophy hunting", a sport of the idle rich.

The ice cave in which Cornelius stored his fresh deer carcasses is now a national park, but people aren't allowed in the cave because of pathogenic organisms, such as salmonella, that live on the blood that soaked into the ice.

Skunks and other small predators entered the cave to gnaw on the ice when food was scarce. They naturally "marked" their territory, until, in the words of Cornelius's grandson, "it smells like a refrigerator that hasn't been cleaned for a thousand years."

Cornelius worked as a "goose herder" on Doctor Glenn's (Hugh J. Glenn, the state's largest wheat grower for which Glenn county is named) ranch. The ranch sat in the middle of Sacramento Valley where ducks and geese migrate in by the thousands from Alaska to spend the winter.

The ranch hired Cornelius to keep the wild geese from ravaging the winter wheat crop. He was paid a dollar a day, plus room and board, and was permitted to shoot and sell as many ducks and geese as he could on the side.

Many people preferred goose to venison and Cornelius didn't have to camp in the cold to get them.

Yearling geese sold for twenty-five cents each, but with his 10-gage shotgun, Cornelius could bag eight or ten geese with a single shot (if they were sitting).

In 1918, it became illegal for hunters to sell wild game to markets. That ended Cornelius' main source of income.

The only thing left was to act as a guide for trophy hunters, but the fact was there were few if any unique animals in California that couldn't be found bigger and better elsewhere.

Cornelius was a friend of "Yankee Jim". Yankee Jim said the "rarest" animal known in Modoc country was "The Giant Spirit Bear," part of a rite of shamanism among the Indians.

It was rarer than the White Medicine Deer of the Maidu, whose skin could be traded for 20 horses. It was even more rare and dangerous than the Sasquach (Bigfoot).

Yankee Jim later became a horse thief and was hung for this offense.

Legend said the Modoc Spirit Bear stood fifteen feet tall on its hind legs and his rear paw print measured twenty inches long. The bear was rumored to be so fast that one dare not turn his back on him.

The claws of the animal were described as being ten inches long and could cut a man in half with a simple flick of its wrist.

The bear had been hunted without success. Cornelius thought that in the springtime, when the snow melts, the Spirit Bear might be seen in a certain alpine meadow near Mt. Lassen.

At 62-years-of age, Cornelius considered getting the bear as the ultimate challenge. He packed his Ford and headed for Mt. Lassen. The plan was to hike in, set up camp in an adjoining valley, and wait for light in a certain rock pile on the downwind side of the meadow.

Cornelius knew that under no circumstances could he go into the meadow itself, where his scent would linger and the wary bear would never show.

He was quiet and in position when the sky began to lighten and the grass was showing through the snow. His gun barrel lay across a log, pointing out over the meadow.

As the stars faded, the dim light revealed a huge black shape against the snow white mountain. It was standing still on its hind legs in the meadow, sniffing the air and looking directly at Cornelius.

The patient hunter aimed just below the ears. The gun kicked, and the echo rolled away, but the bear never moved. Neither did Cornelius move. He waited for dawn.

As the sky lightened, he watched the bear turn more and more into a big burnt tree trunk that looked just like a huge bear on its hind legs.

When Cornelius walked up to the tree, he counted a dozen bullet holes in the trunk. From any other angle but the rock pile from which Cornelius shot, the tree looked less like a bear and more like a tree struck by lightening.

The befuddled hunter had breakfast, packed up his goods, and hiked out. When he returned home, he simply told people that he didn't get one.

Chapter 7

King City

A City Built by A King

The Salinas River wends its way toward Monterey Bay during the summer months.

The Salinas Valley in 1842 was sometimes referred to as "the great Salinas desert." The Salinas River filled its banks in the wintertime, sweeping away anything and everything that might fall in its path.

49

The El Camino hotel was a mainstay in King City. The hotel no longer exists.
(Monterey County Historical Society)

During the summer, the bulging stream of winter drizzled to a trickle. Geologists say the stream goes underground in the summer, wending its way to Monterey Bay.

The San Lorenzo Rancho was the biggest Mexican land grant in the area. Original grantees of the San Lorenzo Rancho were Feliciana Soberanes, who received five leagues of land in 1841. Francisco Rico received a grant of five leagues in 1842.

When Charles King arrived in the Salinas Valley, he recognized its great possibilities as a wheat-growing area. King purchased 13,000 acres from the San Lorenzo grant.

King's neighbors insisted that wheat would never grow on the livestock range, and not very good range at that. If he did harvest a crop, he might never market it.

Hay is being loaded on the Charles King Ranch.
(Monterey County Historical Society)

The only transportation for wheat was the 10-mule-teams that hauled products to Monterey for loading on sailing ships.

King was a friend of Collis P. Huntington, one of the "Big Four" railroad barons. King enticed the Southern Pacific Railroad to extend it line from its present terminus at Soledad south to King's ranch to transport his bountiful wheat crop.

The railroad ran its lines past King's ranch buildings, stubbing out in the middle of a wheat field. J.E. Steinbeck was the first agent for the railroad at its new station. J.E. Steinbeck was the father of John Steinbeck, who wrote of life among the workers of the Salinas Valley with his Grapes of Wrath, East of Eden and Cannery Row books, among others.

Water did come to the area and scenes such as this can be seen up and down the Salinas Valley.

Southern Pacific Milling Company erected a warehouse at the site, an event that gave birth to the town of "King's Station". Soon, a flourmill was built next to the warehouse.

Arriving soon after were seven rail cars loaded with lumber and consigned to William Vanderhurst. The lumber would be used to build the first building in the center of the town, a hardware and general merchandise store.

In 1887, William Mino completed a survey of Kings (now called King City) and the first subdivision was created. The town continued to grow, and in 1897, King sold his large holdings to Spreckels Sugar Company.

William Beebe founded a newspaper there soon after the town's beginnings. It was called the King City Settler. The newspaper died in 1901. Fred Vivian arrived in town soon after and established another newspaper, The Rustler, which survives today.

Vivian was persistent in running editorials calling for the development of water. His foresight was perfect, as it was water that brought life to Salinas Valley's future as a vegetable capital of the west and the world.

Today, the Salinas River runs year round because of the building of two reservoirs, one on the San Antonio River and the other on the Naciemiento River.

Chapter 8

Alcatraz
Island of the Pelicans

No better fortress could be devised to house prisoners than was the barren rock called Alcatraz.

W hen Spanish explorer Juan Manuel de Ayala first mapped the tiny speck of an island, he called it *La Isla de los Alcatraces.* Translated it means Island of the Pelicans.

That is how Alcatraz got its name in the year 1775. It lay barren for the next seventy-two years, when in 1847 the United States Army recognized the strategic value of the "rock" as a military fortification.

In 1853, the U.S. Army began building a military fortification on the island. Included in the construction was the Pacific Coast's first operating lighthouse.

The fortress on Alcatraz became a symbol of United State's military strength. The fortress was equipped with long-range iron cannons and four massive 36,000 pound 15-inch Rodman guns. Each of these guns could sink a hostile ship three miles away.

It was ironic that the island failed to live up to its reputation for firepower. It had only one occasion to fire one 400-pound cannon round at an unidentified ship. The shot missed its target by a wide margin.

The U.S. Army found that Alcatraz was ideal as a long-term prison. The island was isolated and surrounded by frigid waters with hazardous currents.

Alcatraz gained a reputation for being a tough detention facility. Prisoners were separated into three groups based on their conduct and the crimes they had committed.

Prisoners in third class, for instance, were not allowed to have reading material from the library or visits and letters from relatives. A strict rule of silence was enforced at all time.

The Army, citing high operational costs, closed the prison in 1934. Ownership of the facility went to the Department of Justice.

Cellblocks at Alcatraz were stark and cold. Prisoners released from Alcatraz were not likely to want to return.

The Great Depression ushered in a crime wave that aroused the public. People watched in fear as mobsters exerted their influence on metropolitan cities.

Ill-equipped law enforcement agencies likewise cowered before the onslaught of organized crime and its mobsters.

The public's outcry to end the mayhem, brought renewed attention to Alcatraz, considered the ideal lodging place to house this new criminal element. It would not only serve as a housing facility for miscreants, but it would stand as a warning for those with criminal intent.

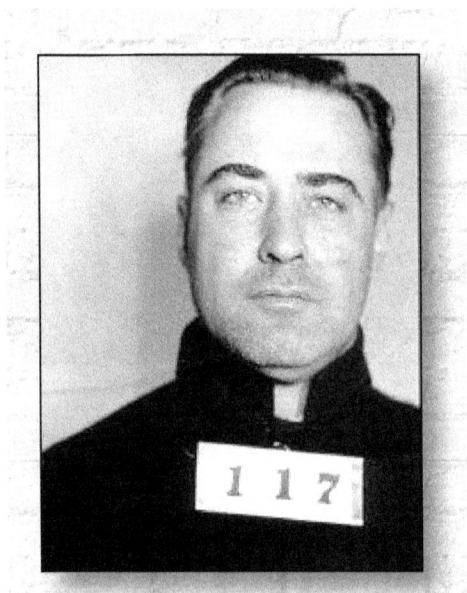

George "Machine Gun" Kelly was one of Alcatraz' most notorious inmates.

In 1934, Alcatraz received a renovation. Electricity was run to each cell, and the walls of utility tunnels were cemented to insure that no criminal could enter or hide in them.

None of the 600 cells in the refurbished prison adjoined any perimeter wall. If an inmate did manage to tunnel through the cell wall, he would still need to find a way to escape from the cell house.

Special tear gas canisters were installed in the ceiling of the dining hall. Guards at various observation points could activate the canisters.

James A. Johnston was appointed warden. His background in business and his twelve years in the Department of Corrections served him well. He was also warden at San Quentin in 1913 and served briefly at Folsom prison.

Johnston had a strong interest in prisoner reform. He didn't believe in chain gangs. Instead, he thought prisoners should report to a job where they would be respected and rewarded for their efforts.

Under Johnston, each prisoner was assigned his own cell. He received only basic necessities, which included food, water, clothing and medical care. The prisoner's contact with the outside world was severed. Prison routine was rigid and unrelenting. As quickly as a given privilege was earned for good behavior, it could be taken away for the slightest infraction.

Warden Johnston met most of the new inmates assigned to Alcatraz. When he saw Al Capone in the lineup, Capone was grinning and making smug comments from the side of his mouth to other inmates.

When it came his turn to approach Johnston, he tried to show off to the other inmates by asking questions on their behalf. The warden handed him his prison number and ordered him back in line.

Capone made several attempts to con the warden out of special privileges, as he had done while incarcerated at the federal prison in Atlanta. The warden rejected all his attempts outright.

Capone finally admitted, "It looks like Alcatraz has got me licked."

Inmates rose at 6:30 a.m., and were allowed twenty-five minutes to tidy their cells and be counted. At 6:55 a.m., they were marched to the mess hall. They had twenty minutes to eat before going to their work assignments.

During its twenty-nine years of operation as a prison, there were fourteen attempted escapes, involving thirty-four inmates. Almost all of the escapees were either recaptured or killed.

Today, Alcatraz is an ecological preserve. It is also home to one of the largest gull colonies on the California coast.

Chapter 9

The Vision of
Ole Hanson

"I vision a place where people can live together more pleasantly than any other place in America. I am going to build a beautiful city on the ocean where the city will be one great park; the architecture will be of all one type, and the homes will be located on sites where nearly everyone will have his wonderful view preserved forever."

The vision of Ole Hanson led to the development of San Clemente.

O le Hanson was fifth of six children born to Norwegian immigrants. He was born in 1874 in the township of Norway, Racine County, Wisconsin.

Ole Hanson never lost his dream to build the perfect city.

Hanson was born into an era that was both reckless and adventurous. The environment of the East and Middle West did not fit his concept of life. Ole Hanson was a builder. Ole wanted to build a beautiful city on coastal California.

"I do not want people repulsed and sent away by an ugliness—as they have been by the ugliness of other communities—I have a clean canvas and I am determined to paint a clean picture."

The young Norwegian worked at many professions. He was a salesman, a legislator, a merchant, a builder, and mayor of Seattle. He amassed three different fortunes, only to lose each one. He never lost his dream for his perfect village along the sea.

While only thirteen, Ole taught school. At seventeen, he worked nights in a clothing store and studied law by day. While still in Racine, he took and passed the bar exam at age nineteen.

State law prevented him from practicing law until he turned twenty-one, so Ole left Racine and went to Chicago. Also at twenty-one, Ole married and became involved in the manufacture of druggists sundries.

A tragic train accident in 1903 left him crippled and partially paralyzed. Doctors warned him he would have trouble walking.

Not Ole Hanson. With his wife and children, he headed for Seattle. Ole walked the entire 2800 miles behind a wagon. The trek gave him back the use of his legs.

In Seattle he operated a successful grocery, but suffered constantly from "itchy feet", always looking for something else. When he investigated the insurance business, he discovered that insurance men did not invest in real estate and Hanson therefore considered it an unsound profession.

In 1908, Hanson ran a vigorous campaign against gambling and vice and was swept into office for the Washington State Legislature. He received the largest margin ever recorded, getting all but ten of the votes cast.

He was elected mayor of Seattle and was credited with breaking the historic strike of 1918.

His wanderlust kept him moving. He went to California and bought land and built houses in the Slausen Tract of Los Angeles. He then moved to Santa Barbara where he invested in the Potter Hotel, which was a financial bonanza.

Ole kept remembering a strip of land he had seen on the California coast while making a train trip from Los Angeles to San Diego a quarter-century before.

Hanson envision what he called his *Spanish Village by the Sea* on that strip of land. The strip was merely five miles long and one-and-one-half mile wide. Ole had envisioned his seaside paradise since he was 26 years old.

He took his idea to the owner of the property, Hamilton H. Cotton. The Los Angeles *Herald Examiner*, on November 8, 1925, carried the story, "...Ole Hanson, subdivider and builder, yesterday announced the founding of a new city."

When the announcement was made, several old friends, investors, former business associates and others joined in for a share of the new development.

Hanson's son, Ole Hanson, Jr. was named director of sales. The son noted that every person his father talked to was converted and bought a piece of the action. Young Hanson wanted to devise a means where his father could talk to thousands, and not just a few.

An early view of San Clemente before it took on the shape envisioned by Old Hanson.

A tent was erected off El Camino and Del Mar. Advertisements ran in every newspaper between Los Angeles and San Diego. The developers then sat back to wait.

Historian Homer Banks, in his book, *The History of San Clemente*, describes the ensuing event:

> "December 6, 1925 started as a day of torture. The big tent was opened. It had rained and the salesmen's cars were parked in ankle deep mud along Avenida del Mar. In the Easley tent house, Hanson waited for the crowd to come.

> "If they came the tent idea would win, if not, San Clemente would win but in another way. Eleven o'clock came. No Cars. No people. More waiting. At eleven-ten, one car, at eleven-thirty, there were twenty-five cars. By high noon 600 people, who had driven an average of 60 miles, filled the tent."

Hanson climbed to the speaker's platform. He was well known for his oratory. But today, he did not attempt to influence the crowd with his verbal brilliance.

"Coldly as an accountant," historian Banks wrote, "Hanson stated the facts of San Clemente, what it cost, why it was chosen for development, the danger of failure, the hope of success, and more—the reason for success. The old time salesmen shivered."

Hanson told the crowd how much he was making on each lot. He let them into the inner secrets of the project. He even let them read his bank statement. He stressed building, building, building. Speculation was attacked. Without a sign of applause, he closed. His salesmen agreed that as a real estate whoopee, it was a flop.

The people, however, responded to Hanson's approach. They understood better than the salesmen what he was saying. That evening, people who listened to Hanson's sincere pitch had purchased $125,000 worth of property.

Ole Hanson, in the depression of the 1930s, lost his own home, which is now called *Casa Romantica*.

These people better understood Hanson than Hanson's first city engineer who was dismayed at the size of Hanson's proposed streets. Hanson called for streets up to eighty-feet wide. Avenida del Mar would be wider than the state highway.

"Let the state catch up," Hanson said.

67

When he submitted the plan to the Orange County Board of Supervisors, it was turned down. To the board, a planned community approach was just too new. The board could not understand dedicating public streets when the state highway wasn't even paved through this section of California.

Still, Hanson's sales crew sold $3,100,000 worth of property in fifteen months and more than $4,600,000 in less than two years.

San Clemente's good fortune did not last. The stock market crash of 1929 and the depression that followed caused many of the residents to lose their homes. Often, they had to move to bigger cities to find employment. The city's population dropped to 250 residents.

Ole Hanson was not exempt from the misfortune. He lost all of his holdings, including his beloved mansion, now known as *Casa Romantica*. Bank of America foreclosed on the property in 1932.

Undaunted, the intrepid Hanson moved on. He created a new community in the desert called *Twenty-Nine Palms*.

Hanson died July 6, 1940 at age 66 from a heart attack. His physician told his family that Ole "worked himself to death." Two hundred fifty friends and relatives went to his Los Angeles home to pay their respects.

Chapter 10

The Sagebrush War

The Roop Fort was built in 1854 and was part of the battle scene when the Sheriff of Plumas County came to sever warrants there. Shots were fired and a few men were injured.

Early settlers believed they lived too far east to be in California. They felt they should be affiliated with the state of Nevada.

The new settlers came to the area by a different route than the pioneers that traveled over the Donner Pass. Of the thousands of people that passed through what is now Lassen County, some chose to remain in the Honey Lake Valley (Now Susanville).

Isaac Roop, founder of Susanville. The town was named for his daughter.

Among these settlers was Isaac Roop, who established a trading post where travelers could stock up with provisions before crossing the Sierra Mountains.

Peter Lassen, leader in the Sagebrush War.

Roop's trading post was first known as Rooptown. It was later named Susanville for Roop's daughter, Susan.

Settlers in Honey Lake Valley were furious when Plumas County officials tried to levy and collect taxes on the residents.

The settlers didn't consider themselves a part of Plumas County, and at the same time, they didn't want to be a part of the Territory of Utah—a vast region that included what would become several western states.

The Nevada Territorial Legislature was determined to keep Honey Lake Valley under its jurisdiction. On December 2, 1862, the Nevada legislature changed Lake County, Nevada's name, to Roop County.

The name change was to honor Isaac Roop, who in 1859 served as the first provisional governor of the Territory of Nevada.

71

This action invited troubles from California officials. When Plumas County officials attempted to arrest Roop, it started what is known as the Sagebrush War.

Isaac Roop and Peter Lassen led an effort to form a separate territory—one they would call Nataqua. The name Nataqua is an Indian word meaning "woman" or "wife".

This caused a conflict of authority. Plumas County officials claimed the right to exercise jurisdiction over the territory embraced within the limits of what the Nevada Legislature had organized into the County of Roop.

A Plumas County judge enjoined a Justice of the Peace from holding court in Roop County. When the justice refused to obey, he was fined $100 for contempt of court.

Plumas County's sheriff and his deputy traveled to Roop to arrest the Roop sheriff and the Roop County judge. Roop citizens decided they had had enough.

They took the prisoners from the custody of Plumas County officials. Plumas County Sheriff E.H. Pierce returned with a posse of Plumas citizens estimated at some one hundred to one hundred-eighty persons. In addition, they brought one piece of artillery with them.

Roop County forces gathered in what is called Roop's Fort, and Plumas fighters took possession of a barn in the neighborhood. During the fighting, Roop riflemen shot and wounded one Plumas posse member. Plumas fighters wounded two of the men in Roop's fort.

An armistice was agreed upon calling for a halt to fighting and a solution to the hostilities. A committee of Honey Lake Valley and Plumas County officials convened in Susanville.

Both sides agreed to disband their forces. Plumas County Sheriff E.H. Pierce would take the case to the Governor of California, asking him to confer with the Governor of Nevada.

It was agreed that a party composed of both California and Nevada surveyors would survey the boundary, settling the issue once and for all.

It was determined in 1863 that Honey Lake Valley was indeed in the state of California. The following year, the County of Lassen was created and Roop County ceased to exist.

The survey team left the eastern portion of Honey Lake Valley in Washoe County, Nevada.

There were other boundary disputes between the two states. Nevada's western boundary line was not easily established with statehood.

Instead of simply stating that the new territory's western boundary would be the eastern boundary of California, the Nevada Organic Act specified that the boundary between California and the proposed territory would be the "dividing ridge separating the waters of the Carson Valley from those that flow into the Pacific."

That would make the boundary the crest of the Sierra Nevada. California never agreed to the Sierra Nevada ridge as the dividing boundary.

One reason was that it appeared the mineral discoveries at Aurora might actually lie in California. At the time, both Esmeralda County,

Nevada, and Mono County, California both claimed Aurora.

Aurora, at one time or another, served as the county seat of both counties. Aurora had one courthouse and two sets of county officers. In 1862, an election was held in Aurora to select officials for the two counties, one set for Esmeralda, in Nevada, and the other for Mono, in California. There were separate polling places but the same voters.

Unlike the Roop County affair, up to the time the survey team ascertained the border of California and Nevada, Aurora seemed to exist peacefully in both states.

When the joint California-Nevada survey team determined that Roop County was actually part of California, it likewise held that Aurora was a part of Nevada.

Mono County then moved its county seat to Bridgeport, California, settling the issue.

Chapter 11

He Kept the Bank Open

Amadeo Peter Giannini

madeo Peter Giannini rushed to his
Bank of Italy in downtown San
Francisco. He was unsure what he would
find at his bank in the wake of the 1906 earthquake
that shook him out of bed.

In a borrowed produce wagon, Giannini rushed
to his Bank of Italy, which he founded two years
earlier. He and some employees emptied the bank's
vault, loading two million dollars in gold, coins and
securities onto the borrowed produce wagon.

The banker concealed his rich wagonload of gold and coins with a layer of vegetables to throw off potential robbers.

Other San Francisco bankers elected to stay closed during the days following the earthquake, allowing them to sort out the damage.

Not Giannini. He placed wooden planks across two barrels on the docks near San Francisco's North Beach to serve as a desk. He opened for business to extend credit to small businesses and individuals in need of money to start over.

Nine days after the quake, a newspaper advertisement announced the location of his bank's operation. He became known as the son of immigrants who loaned money to immigrants when other bankers refused. His western banking empire created a system of branch banks to serve ordinary people.

His actions in 1906 are credited with spurring San Francisco's recovery following the tremor and the fire that ravaged the city.

A.P. Giannini was the son of Italian immigrants. He was born in San Jose in 1870. A disgruntled employee killed his father over a dollar debt when Amadeo was seven years of age.

His mother later married Lorenzo Scatena, a teamster who then entered the produce business. Giannini left school at age 14 to assist him. The business thrived, its success based on the impeccable reputation for integrity that Giannini exuded.

At age 31, he announced that he was selling his half-interest in the business to his employees and retiring. He once said, "I don't want to be rich. No man actually owns a fortune. It owns him."

This is a branch of the Bank of Italy in Santa Paula in 1925.

Banks that maintained a policy of lending only to wealthy clients angered Giannini. He opened his Bank of Italy in a San Francisco saloon in 1904, determined to serve the little fellow.

Giannini had ample opportunity to live up to his philosophy when the 1906 earthquake shook the city to pieces. Giannini would loan customers money based on nothing but a signature.

When he opened his bank in 1904, he offered those potential customers that were ignored by other bankers the opportunity to open savings accounts and get loans.

Within a year, deposits with his Bank of Italy were soaring above $700,000, a hefty amount by current standards. He courted immigrants from the Yugoslavian, Russian, Mexican, Portuguese, Chinese, Greek and other communities. By the mid-1920s, he owned the third largest bank in the nation.

A major portion of the bank's first day deposits came from small tradesmen who had been actively solicited by Giannini and other members of the bank. Often, a depositor's ignorance of English or bank procedure required that the bank's personnel fill out deposit slips and checks.

Giannini viewed the earthquake as offering an opportunity for his Bank of Italy. His personal knowledge of his customers' accounts allowed him to resume operations quickly.

In less than six weeks following the earthquake, deposits in the Bank of Italy exceeded withdrawals.

When, in mid-1907 Giannini heard rumblings of a financial downturn despite the nation's apparent prosperity at the present time, he took action. He began increasing his bank's gold reserves, urged customers to increase their deposits while at the same time reducing their outstanding loans.

When the financial panic did hit, Giannini's bank was in position to tackle the financial collapse head-on. The Bank of Italy did not have to invoke rules limiting withdrawals or requiring advance notice before withdrawals as competing banks did.

Giannini's greatest accomplishment may have been the institution of branch banking. He studied the branch banking situation occurring in Canada. When California enacted a law in 1909 allowing branch banking, Giannini was already ahead of the game.

Directors of the Bank of Italy authorized opening such a bank in San Jose on Columbus Day, 1909. By 1918, the Bank of Italy became the first statewide branch banking system in the U.S., with 24 branches throughout California.

In the late 1920s, Giannini approached Orra E. Monnette, president and founder of the Los Angeles based Bank of America. The Los Angeles bank exhibited strong growth as a result of developing an advanced bank branching system

Giannini's Bank of Italy merged with Monnette's Bank of America in 1929. They used The Bank of America as the name of their joint operation, and Giannini and Monnette served as co-chairs of the new bank.

Giannini died in 1949 at age 79. By the time of his death, Bank of America was California's largest, the nation's largest, and the world's largest commercial and savings bank.

Chapter 12

A River With A Cause

The Cosumnes River is the only undammed stream originating in the Sierra.
(Jason May, US Geological Survey)

The Cosumnes River is a short little river. Compared to other streams cascading down the Sierra, it is far more significant to the casual viewer than is revealed on the surface.

The river is just eighty miles long, but gets its importance from two aspects. First, it is the only undammed river originating on the western slope of the Sierra.

Second, it provides scientists and other investigators, such as bird watchers, with a wealth of information. Its real significance occurs once it reaches California's Central Valley where it merges with the Mokelumne River.

The little river's headwaters begin at the eight thousand foot level in the Sierra Nevada. Its main water source is rain, but it does get a smattering of snowmelt before it undertakes it meandering route down the mountainside.

The Cosumnes River was named in the same way the Mokelumne and Tuolumne Rivers were. The *umne* suffix means "people of". The *cos* suffix means salmon or fish.

Before descending to the Central Valley, rock climbers find the Cosumnes River Gorge challenging. New climbers can learn their craft in the rocky gorge while seasoned rock climbers can hone their skills to peak condition.

Climbers are warned that each person is responsible for his own safety, as it is not patrolled. It is doubtful that a cell-phone signal can penetrate to the outside, and should an accident happen, it could take hours for a rescue party to arrive. A rescue by helicopter is deemed difficult if not impossible.

The Bureau of Land Management (BLM) publicly owns and manages the Cosumnes River

Gorge. The American River Conservancy donated sixty-one acres of the gorge to BLM.

The Cosumnes River is a small stream that overruns its banks during winter storms. With no dams blocking their path, Chinook salmon and Pacific lamprey make their way upstream to spawn.

Two decades ago, The Nature Conservancy, (TNC) recognized the changing character of the Central Valley landscape. Farmland was converted to development. Land that wasn't going to development was being upgraded to a higher cash use, such as vineyards.

Sandhill cranes spend September to March at the Cosumnes River Preserve.

TNC purchased its first parcel along the Cosumnes in 1984. It contained 85 acres of virgin valley oak. Ducks Unlimited, a nonprofit group dedicated to conserving, restoring and managing wetlands, then purchased another 320 acres.

In 1987, the two organizations established the 1000 acre Cosumnes River Preserve. Since then, the preserve has grown to almost 50,000 acres as additional partners and donors make contributions. The Bureau of Land Management manages the preserve.

The Cosumnes River Preserve includes wetlands, agricultural fields, grassland, and valley oak riparian woodland. The American Bird Conservancy has designated the preserve as a globally important bird area. (Cosumnes River Preserve)

Observers have recorded more than 200 species of birds in and around the preserve. The preserve is a sanctuary for many migratory birds and provides protection for rare reptiles and mammals, such as the endangered giant garter snake and the elusive river otter.

In a three-mile stretch of the Cosumnes River, wild grapes and blackberries run riot, along with cottonwoods and valley oak trees they provide a welcome shelter from the blistering sun.

A hundred years ago, such a riverbank with its tangle of trees and vines was a common site in the central valley. Today, only one-tenth of one percent of California's riparian forests remain.

The luxurious nature of the forest is water-born. The undammed Cosumnes River still floods in the winter and spring. The rushing waters carry with it silt that is deposited in the lowlands where it meets with the Tuolumne.

The Cosumnes River Preserve has fresh-water marshes that host a concentration of sand-hill cranes, as well as Canada and Ross's geese. Many species of ducks use the preserve as a migratory habitat.

Some 30,000 people visit the preserve each year. More than 5,000 students studying conservation of both land and animals use the preserve.

Education and recreation includes hiking, bird watching, canoeing, and kayaking.

Preserve managers still fear encroaching urban development on its pristine area. The Cosumnes River Preserve is recognized as one of California's most significant natural areas.

Visitors can travel through a tidal swamp of willows and button willows. One may find it necessary to climb over fallen trees, scramble through wild blackberry patches, and duck under low limbs. The trip is made worthwhile by the singing and chirping of 70 to 80 species of birds.

Wild grape and poison oak are prominent features in the park. There are patches of exotic trees, including figs and pears in the forest.

The Cosumnes River Preserve provides a look at the way much of California's Central Valley looked before man disturbed nature.

Chapter 13

He Left
Civilization Behind

Marshal and Tanya South built this home of handmade adobe bricks on Ghost Mountain. Here, two of their children, Rudyard and Rider, who typically wear no clothes, are pictured.

Marshal and Tanya South left the ordered civilization in which they grew up to live atop a waterless mountain in the Anza-Borrego Desert.

Marshall South

They came close to living off the fat of the land, collecting cactus fruit and yucca leaves as part of their food staples. They ground their own wheat to make bread. They wore clothing only when they expected company.

For the next seventeen years, Marshal and Tanya wrote poetry and philosophical articles. Marshal wrote a monthly column in the *Desert Sun,* describing his family's life in the desert wilderness.

The articles provided enough income to keep Marshal and his family in meager supplies which he purchased in the town of Julian.

They called their adobe home *Yaquitepec.* A portion of the name is after *Yaqui,* the fierce freedom-loving Indians of Sonora, Mexico, and *tepec,* referring to the hill. The hill itself they called *Ghost Mountain.*

Marshal South's disenchantment with civilized society developed early in life but really came to fruition while serving in the army.

He was born Roy Bennett Richards on February 24, 1889 near Adelaide, South Australia. His father, William Charles Bennett Richards, was born in the U.S., but his mother was born in Australia.

His father owned and managed large sheep ranches in Australia and was able to send his son to prestigious schools. He sent son Roy to St. Peter's College, one of South Australia's finest. While a student, Roy began writing various pieces of prose, poetry, fiction, humor, satire and commentary on political and social issues.

His mother divorced his father and took her sons, Roy and Norman, to the United States. She settled in Oceanside, California, using the Richards family name. Young Roy was already a published writer, his work having been published in the *Port Augusta Dispatch.*

When he arrived on the California coast, Roy adopted the pen name of Benjamin and dropped the name of Roy. The *Los Angeles Tribune* published one of his poems on May 7, 1912 under that name.

He then began using the pen name Marshal South on articles he sold to the *Oceanside Blade.* His poetry and writings were winning high praise. *The Los Angeles Tribune* in particular noted that Marshal South's poem "Progress" was "Being complimented and copied widely."

Marshal was drafted into the army in 1914 at age 27. While stationed in Douglas, Arizona, he met and married Margaret Frieda Schweichler, a civilian secretary working in the same office as South worked.

The couple had a son, Marshal, Jr. Shortly after South was discharged from the army, Margaret asked him to leave. Marshal was never interested in making or saving money while she was both practical and ambitious.

This sent Marshal into a funk of depression. He moved back to Oceanside and took a job as a carpenter for the Rosicrucian Fellowship. There he met Tanya, who worked as a secretary. The two married soon after.

Tanya South

They struggled to make ends meet. They made frequent camping trips into the desert, exploring the country in the Anza-Borrego area.

In 1930, the couple decided to drop out of organized society. In an article he wrote for the *Saturday Evening Post* South expounded on their reasons for moving away from civilization.

They did not want to be slaves to making money and they wanted to pursue more creative and spiritual endeavors. They selected *Ghost Mountain* as the site of the home they would build.

There was no water on the mountain. When the Souths built *Yaquitepec*, Marshal engineered an extensive water system. He built catch basins to gather the rainfall, and cisterns in which to store it.

There was no electricity or other artificial sources of light and very little fuel available for a stove on the sparse desert. It was a rugged climb up the one-mile trail to their house. As a consequence, the South's had few visitors.

Marshal soon resubmitted a few manuscripts that had been rejected by editors. A London publisher published four of his books, "Flame of Terrible Valley," "Child of Fire", "Juanita of the Border Country", and "Gunsight."

But the Book of Nature—the same one that the Indian studied so successfully—still is available free to all. And the Desert Edition of it, whose pages we on Ghost Mountain ruffle through every day by the aid of the wind and sunshine, always provides interesting items and food for thought.

(Marshal South)

One of his articles in the *Saturday Evening Post* led to a contract with *Desert Magazine* to write a one-year series on what it was like for the couple and their children on top of an arid desert mountain.

Marhall and Tanya were nudists when there were no visitors.

The South's three children included Rider Del Sol South, Rudyard Del Sol South, and Victoria Del Sol South. The children were all born in Oceanside and Tanya spent her last month of pregnancy there for each birth.

Readers enjoyed Marshal's articles so much he was soon dubbed *The Desert Prophet.*

In his writings, South focused only on the positive aspects of the life that he, Tanya and his children led on Ghost Mountain. Despite the glowing life Marshal described in his columns, the family's actual existence looked very different.

According to Rider South, the oldest son, "They fought like cats and dogs." Tanya felt trapped on the mountain, and worried that her children needed to adapt to a civilized life while they still could.

In October 1946, Tanya walked her children three miles, where she flagged down a vehicle to carry a letter to San Diego.

The letter was a plea for help. The Red Cross responded and provided her transportation to San Diego. A San Diego newspaper headlined her action: "Divorce Plea Breaks Up Hermit Family."

A judge gave custody of the children to Tanya and ordered Marshal to provide financial support for his family. He was told to bring food and supplies to the house once each week.

Marshal did not contest the divorce.

Marshal South died on October 22, 1948, at 59-years-of-age.

Chapter 14

Indian Pollution Found

A steam shovel demolishes the Emeryville shell mound in 1924 to make way for a paint factory.

Even before the white man arrived in California, some disturbing things were happening between Mother Nature and the Native Indians.

An outspoken researcher at the University of Utah says that all was not necessarily well with California and Indian ecology.

California, in the 1700s and the 1800s, was rife with birds, elk, deer, marine mammals and other wildlife. Wild geese and waterfowl were plentiful.

Indians were credited with maintaining a close relationship with nature and fostering its flora and fauna.

Jack Broughton

But Professor Jack Broughton, associate professor of anthropology, University of Utah, points a finger at some of their practices.

Broughton spent seven years—from 1997 to 2004— pawing through 5,736 bird bones found in an ancient Native American garbage dump on the shores of San Francisco Bay.

From a time long before Europeans arrived, Native Americans lived around the Emeryville Shell Mound. It was the materials from this mound that Broughton used for his research. The mound at one time measured over 60-feet high and 350 feet in diameter.

Native Americans constructed the shell mound by throwing shells from the catches of shellfish. One source notes the Indians also used it as a resting site for their dead.

Broughton determined the species of every bone, or when that wasn't possible, at least the family. He then used the bones to reconstruct a portrait of the human bird-hunting behavior spanning nineteen hundred years.

Broughton concluded that from 2,600 to at least 700 years ago, native people hunted some species to extinction. Wildlife numbers returned to abundant numbers only after European diseases decimated Indian populations starting in the 1500s.

It wasn't just birds which declined during these periods. Broughton found population declines in fish, such as sturgeon, and in mammals such as elk. Professor Broughton believes the Indians were over-hunting

Biologists have assumed that the abundant wildlife in California of 200 years ago existed for thousands of years. This assumption has been used to make decisions on how to manage and conserve endangered or threatened species.

"California has been viewed as a kind of utopia or a land of milk and honey, a super-rich natural environment," said Broughton. He says his study challenges that assumption. The Native Americans were not always the healthy, happy people they were made out to be before the arrival of the white man.

"Depending on when and where you look back in time, native peoples were either living in harmony with nature or eating their way through a vast array of large-sized, attractive prey species."

Broughton is a Californian himself, growing up in Camarillo. While earning his bachelor's and master's degrees at California State University, Chico, he studied bones from archaeological sites in California's Sacramento Valley.

He began to recognize that early natives had a strong impact on elk, deer, and sturgeon—"anything big and juicy", he said.

Emeryville was the largest of 425 shell mounds identified along the San Francisco Bay by 1900. It was made up of distinct layers, which allowed dating of its bones.

In 1902, 1906, and 1924, scientists excavated thousands from the shell mound, recording the layer in which each bone was found. The bones from the shell mound were stored for decades at the Phoebe Apperson Hearst Museum of Anthropology at the University of California, Berkeley.

Broughton analyzed 5,736 bones, a task he characterized as a "labor of love".

"It's a real challenge when you've got a broken bird bone and it could be any of 100 species. It may take hours or a day to identify a single bone. So you can imagine the excitement when you finally nail it," he said.

His research revealed that bones from the Emeryville shell mound represented 64 species: 45 species of water birds, including ducks, geese, cormorants, and shorebirds; 15 species of raptors such as red-tailed hawks and bald eagles; and two species each from the groups that include grouse and quail, and crows and ravens.

His laborious counting showed that the bird population diminished throughout the 1,900-year period represented by the shell mound. Species with the most significant reductions were those that were most attractive to hunters.

As nearby food sources diminished, native peoples increasingly hunted birds at greater distances and depleted their populations. After depleting larger shorebirds, natives hunted smaller shorebirds such as sandpipers.

Broughton said he concluded that native peoples depressed bird populations only after he examined possible alternative causes.

Europeans arrived in the 1500s and infected Native Americans with fatal diseases such as smallpox, malaria, and influenza. There was a resulting decline of as much as 90 percent in the Indian population.

Hunting pressure on wildlife diminished and geese and ducks and other birds became abundant again. "You could kill them with a club or stick," Broughton said.

Many scientists view negative effects on bird populations as modern phenomenon, said John Faaborg, editor of Ornithological monographs and a wildlife biology professor at University of Missouri-Columbia.

Faaborg says, "Now we need to reconsider our impressions about human impacts on bird populations in the distant past. Jack Broughton makes an excellent case that native peoples living in the San Francisco bay area harvested enough birds to deplete populations and even cause some extinction."

History works its magic again.

Chapter 15

The Modoc Indian War

This drawing by William Simpson depicts the stronghold of Captain Jack in the lava beds around Tule Lake. (Library of Congress)

I t was a war that didn't need to happen. The federal government first set aside an ill-suited reservation in Southern Oregon on which to herd the Modocs and the Klamaths.

Government officials erred in placing the Modoc and the Klamath tribes on the same reservation. They were enemies. When the Modocs arrived at the government's designated reservation for them, the bullying Klamaths regarded them as intruders

The Klamath Indians outnumbered the Modocs and were relentless in their harassment. Making matters worse, the government did not live up to the promises it made when it put the Modocs on the reservation.

Modoc Chief Captain Jack.

Government officials broke their promises to supply the Modoc people with adequate rations. The Modocs were located in an unfavorable place with little opportunity to survive on the resources around them. This is considered the main factor that led to the Modoc War.

The Modoc Indians spurned the reservation site and retreated to the lava beds. This embarrassed Army officials, who were dedicated to corralling the Modocs on the proposed reservation, suitable or not.

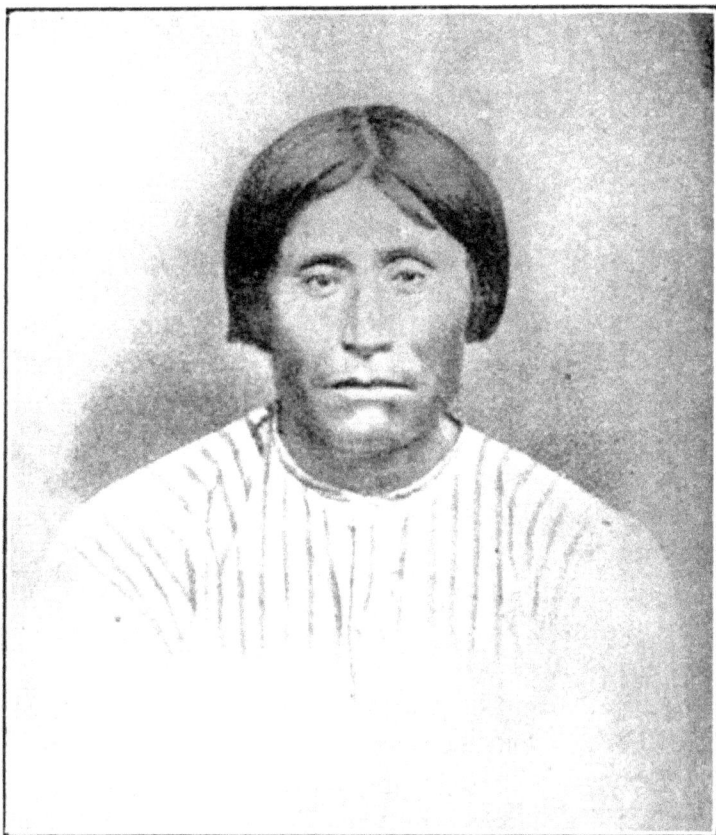

Captain Jack

Modoc leader, *Kientepoos* (Captain Jack) recognized that the Indians at least had a chance of defending themselves in the lava beds.

Captain Jack and about sixty Modoc Indians took refuge in the rough terrain of the lava field. The Army was adamant. The Indians must return to their reservation in southern Oregon.

Led by Lt. Col. Frank Wheaton, soldiers stormed the Indian stronghold on a cold, blustery dawn in January 1873.

Wheaton wrote to General Edward Camby:

We will be prepared to make short work of this impudent and enterprising savage.

There were almost 350 soldiers ready to attack Captain Jack's 60 warriors. Wheaton's battle strategy was a two-pronged advance, one from the east and one from the west.

He was certain the Modocs would surrender when caught in the pincers of the advancing soldiers.

What General Wheaton had not counted on was that his forces would be attacking the wily Modocs through dense, icy fog. The fog was so dense that Wheaton could not use the howitzers waiting on the bluff above them for fear of hitting his own men.

The western unit moved within a mile of the Modocs. Soldiers approaching from the east crawled along the lava beds until they reached a collapsed lava tube.

From here, the soldiers fired random shots in the general direction of Captain Jack and his defenders.

The Modoc's position in the lava beds was impenetrable.
(Google Images)

The Indians, under the skillful leadership of Captain Jack, made it appear that their numbers were far greater than they were. Two or three Indian riflemen could pin down a squad of soldiers until other Modocs from other positions rushed to send a barrage of shots at the soldiers.

Through the long day, the persistent Indians shattered the morale of the soldiers. "How could they fight an enemy they could not see?

Bloody battling continued through the day with the Modocs reaping severe casualties on the army forces. The battle to rout the Indians resulted in thirty-seven army casualties and no Modoc losses. At 5 p.m., January 17, 1873, General Wheaton ordered his troops to retreat.

In a report on the battle, Wheaton wrote:

> *I have never before encountered an enemy, civilized or savage, occupying a position of such natural strength—nor have I ever seen troops engage a better-armed or more skillful foe.*

Captain Rueben F. Bernard, commander of Troop G., which formed one of the pincer forces coming in on Captain Jack's position, wrote:

> *Many of the men would rather serve ten years in Alcatraz than attack the enemy again in the lava beds.*

This victory reinforced the Modoc's position at discussing a peace treaty. Many peace treaty talks followed and Captain Jack remained firm in his insistence on a Lost River reservation. The U.S. government refused.

It was becoming obvious to army officials in Washington that it was less costly to feed an Indian than to fight him. Yet, peace negotiations dragged on for months.

Finally, two of Captain Jack's warriors, Hooker Jim and Curly-Headed Doctor (medicine man) convinced their chief that the only alternative was to kill the Peace Commissioners.

When General Canby refused to withdraw his troops from the lava beds where the Indians were ensconced during a negotiating session, Captain Jack signaled his warriors to shoot. Canby and Reverend Eleazar Thomas fell to their death. This ended any chance of a negotiated settlement.

While the Modoc Indian conflict has been overshadowed by other Indian battles such as Custer's attack at Little Big Horn and the Nez Perce and Apache Rebellions, the Modoc War may have been the most ruthless.

It was the encroachment of white settlers in the beginning that brought on the wrath of the Indians. The white men were taking over the rich farmlands and insisting that the "hostile" Indians be moved to a reservation.

The outnumbered Modocs did resign themselves to live on a reservation in Oregon. There, they were again forced to exist with the Klamath Indians, their mortal enemies.

After repeated differences with the bullying Klamaths, Captain Jack took half of the Modoc tribe to return to the tribe's former territory on Lost River in southern Oregon.

Again the white settlers protested, asking the Army to place the Indians on a reservation.

Peace talks between the Army and the Modocs were arranged to prevent further bloodshed. Winema "Toby" Riddle, cousin to Captain Jack and the wife of a white man, acted as interpreter. She warned officers of the hostile nature of some of Captain Jack's warriors.

Within three days, the Army moved mortars and howitzers into the field, and within three more days, the Modocs began a retreat that forced them to surrender.

The Army hung Captain Jack and three other leaders for the murders of Canby and Thomas and the remainder of the tribe was exiled to far-off Okalahoma.

Chapter 16

Girl Stolen by Indians

(The following first person account tells the ordeal of Mrs. A. Thankful Carson. It is horrifying in its intensity. A brave girl tells of her two brothers being killed before she herself escaped from Indian captors. The story was printed in the Dogtown Territorial Quarterly, published in Paradise, California.)

She was nine years old when it happened. She, her two brothers, Jimmy, age 11, and Johnny, age 6, were walking home from school. They were the children of Samuel and Mary Ann Lewis, who moved to the Oroville area in 1853.

Little Dry Creek was a tempting place for youngsters to quench their thirst. The stream flowed through an inviting oak grove. The water seemed cooler and more refreshing there.

Out of the quiet surrounding the Little Dry Creek came a shot. It hit little Jimmy in the back. He pitched forward into the stream.

Four Indians emerged from behind a tall grape vine growing along the stream. They pelted the inert body of little Jimmy lying in the steam with rocks, making sure he was dead.

Six other Indians joined the first four. One had one big foot and one small foot. The others called him Big Foot. He donned Jimmy's hat, which was made of Calico and adorned with a red flower.

Mrs. A. Thankful Carson at nine-years-of age was kidnapped by Indians and escaped.
(Dogtown Territorial Enterprise)

This is the ordeal that Mrs. A. Thankful Carson, recalled years later.

One Indian grabbed her by the arm, while another took a firm hold on Johnny. "We left the valley and went up the mountainside. I asked the Indians to let me go home, but they said, 'No, we are going to take you to our home, your home no more.'"

Both Mrs. Carson and her brother Johnny were barefoot, yet the Indians prodded them along. A neighbor, John Leonard and another neighbor came along the road in a wagon.

The Indians hustled the children into the brush, placing a hand over their mouths to prevent their yelling to the men in the wagon.

At one point, the Indians forced the girl to walk on her tiptoes so her trail could not be traced. They carried the boy. That night, they camped under a grove of trees. An Indian slept next to the two youngsters.

When they woke, young Johnny started to cry. Four Indians took him back into the woods. I was forced to proceed with the others. "I asked the Indians if I could go back and kiss my brother," Mrs. Carson said. "They said no, and jabbed me with their guns."

Soon, the four Indians who took the boy rejoined them. Mrs. Carson asked, "What did you do with Johnny?"

"He's all right," they said.

"No, you have killed him, I know you have."

The Indians still denied it but she remained confident she was right.

She soon spotted one of the Indians wearing some of her brother's clothes, including his little cap. "Then I was positive they had killed him." The Indians still denied it.

"I had a pair of gold earrings which I wore," Mrs. Carson related. "Two Indians wanted them

111

and caught hold of my ears to tear them out. Don't I said, I will give them to you."

She handed one to each Indian, which caused them to argue because each of them wanted both earrings.

Her feet bare, Mrs. Carson walked over rocks and brush causing her feet to bleed and ache. At one point, the group left a lone Indian to guard her along the trail.

She begged him to stop so she could rest. The Indian was carrying a quarter of beef they killed on a ranch along the way and he, too, was tired. We came to a large rock and he consented to stop.

"I told him to take the beef and the guns to the other Indians and let me rest on this rock, and then I will travel good with you."

"All right, but if you move from this rock I will kill you." The Indians, Mrs. Carson noted, spoke good English.

As the Indian moved away, Mrs. Carson crouched behind the rock. She raised her head above the stone and the Indian pointed his gun in a threatening move.

She moved back onto the rock.

He soon walked on, disappearing in the woods. When she thought her way was clear, Mrs. Carson took action.

"I rolled over and off the rock into the ravine, then got up and ran backwards toward Big Chico Creek for over a mile, passed by an old cabin, and ran through thistles with my bare feet and out of the path so the Indians could not track me."

Once, the Indians passed within a hundred yards of her as she hid in the bushes. When she could no longer hear them, Mrs. Carson crawled out of her hiding place and waded the creek.

She finally came to Mrs. Thomasson's place, where she saw two men working in a field. One was Nath Thomasson, who went forward to meet her.

Seeing her condition, he picked her up and carried her to the house. Mrs. Thomasson washed and greased the little girl's feet and picked out all the stickers and briars and gave her something to eat.

"My mother and grandmother had found Johnny's body before the news of the kidnapping reached them," she said.

Mrs. Carson was able to guide a posse to the location where Jimmy was killed. Jimmy's body was stripped naked and his skull was crushed. Some men stayed with the body while others returned to Mr. Nance's place.

There, they selected the best boards from the barn and made a neat coffin for Jimmy's body. Mrs. Nance provided sheets in which to wrap the corpse.

He was buried next to Johnny in the Clear Creek graveyard.

Chapter 17

Gold in Southern California

Prospectors work in Placerita Canyon in early 1840s.

Southern Californians are relentless in claiming the original gold discovery in California.

That is rightfully so, as it was in Placerita Canyon that Mexican vaquero Jose Francisco de Gracia Lopez made his startling discovery. Later, Placerita Canyon became famous for another find, "white oil".

An old poster advertises the site of California's first gold discovery.

Lopez supervised the livestock operation for ranch owner Antonio del Valle. Del Valle's wife, Dona Jacoba, was the niece of Lopez. Governor Juan Batista Alvarado granted del Valle eight square leagues (48,612 acres) in the upper Santa Clara River valley for his meritorious service in the military.

When he left to inspect the ranch's livestock, Dona Jacoba asked Lopez to bring back some wild onions. At noontime, Lopez was deep in Cañon de los Encinos (Live Oak Canyon).

Lopez selected a spot under a huge oak tree for he and his helper to have lunch and a siesta. After his siesta, Lopez took his knife and dug up some nearby wild onions.

There were gold flakes clinging to the roots of the wild onions. This caused Lopez and other ranch employees to scour the valley's riverbanks. They found more gold.

They took the ore to Los Angeles for assaying. The Philadelphia Mint tested the gold at .926 fine.

Word of the gold spread through the region. Hundreds of prospectors flocked to Live Oak Canyon. The canyon became known as *Placerita Canyon*, meaning "Placer", for surface deposits of gold.

During the years 1842 to 1847, miners gleaned some thirteen hundred pounds of gold from Placerita Canyon.

Many accounts of the southern California gold find describe Lopez as a simple vaquero who stumbled onto the gold. Francisco Lopez was no ordinary vaquero. He studied at the famous *Colegio de Mineria* in Mexico City and learned the techniques of prospecting and mining.

Placerita Canyon became noted as well for its production of "white oil". The white oil was exhibited at the 1876 World's Fair.

The oil was as clear as kerosene and able to burn 100 times longer than conventional oil.

"Wild cat" oil drillers began prospecting the Newhall area of Los Angeles County in the 1850s. San Fernando Mission was using natural oil that it crudely distilled to fire its lamps.

When tested, the Placerita Canyon oil proved to be 83 percent gasoline and was put directly into early engines to make them run.

As a teenager, George Starbuck would take a five-gallon can to his great uncle Tom Walker's white oil well, fill it up and pour the oil directly into his Model A Ford.

Later, when another well was drilled, Starbuck's grandfather laid pipes and hooked into the natural gas line. The gas was used to light natural gas lamps in his home. The lamps and the burners on the natural gas stove burned twenty-four hours a day.

Historians believe a natural filtration system existed in the San Gabriel Fault Zone. It is believed that the movement of the oil through the fine sands and clay of the San Gabriel Fault Zone resulted in the clear kerosene-like oil.

Chapter 18

St. George's Reef Light

St. George's Light warned ships of the dangerous *Dragon Rocks* near Crescent City.

English explorer George Vancouver christened the hazardous reef off Point St. George as *Dragon Rocks*. Over time, the reef became known as St. George Reef.

Waves crash most of the time against the 300-ft rock supporting St. George's Light. Keepers detested duty at the light.

Two hundred fifteen lives on the side-wheeler *Brother Jonathan* were lost at the reef in 1865. The public clamor required the Lighthouse Board do something about the dangerous impediment.

Engineers could not decide where to build a light at St. George's Point. The wave-swept reef itself provided little area on which to locate a lighthouse.

Difficult weather only allowed surveyors to get to the rocks three times over a four-week period. In 1883, engineers attached a cable between the rocks and a schooner.

On the cable was a cage in which to move workers to the rock, and if need be, remove them just as quickly if a storm threatened.

The construction came at great cost. At first, $100,000 was allocated, to build the $330,000 project. Work was suspended in 1885 for lack of funds.

In 1887, $120,000 more was appropriated. When the light was finally completed, the total cost was $704,633.78. It was the most expensive lighthouse ever built in the U.S.

Six-man teams manned the lighthouse. Lighthouse keepers detested duty at St. George Reef Light. The tower was cold and inhospitable, and storms were frequent. Relief workers only arrived when the weather was favorable.

One group of keepers was stranded on the rock for 59 days in 1937. The men had been solid friends for years but would not speak to one another nor face each other when eating after being on the rock.

The *Keeper's Log* notes that once the weather let up and other workers replaced the men, their animosity toward each other lessened and returned to normal.

The lighthouse stands 146 feet high and is the tallest on the Pacific coast. The lighthouse was built on a small rock only 300 feet in diameter, and is one of the most exposed lighthouses along the coast.

The base of the tower is a solid block of concrete and granite, and the tower above is built of granite blocks. The stone for the lighthouse was quarried from granite boulders found on Mad River near Humboldt Bay.

Living quarters and the light tower were housed in the same structure at St. George Reef Light. At other lighthouses, living quarters consisted of a separate cottage.

Several people died during construction of the lighthouse. Dozens of workers resigned or sought transfer. Some even suffered mental breakdowns.

The lighthouse was decommissioned and replaced by a buoy in 1975.

Chapter 19

California's State Flower

The California poppy earned its royal seat as California's State Flower. When the California State Floral Society voted to select a state flower in 1890, there were three nominees.

They included *Eschscholzia californica*, the California poppy, *Romneya coulteri*, the giant poppy, and *Calochortus* the California lily (no species indicated).

The California poppy won all but three votes, and those three were cast for the California lily. The giant poppy received no votes at all.

Juan Rodriguez Cabrillo sailed up the California coast in 1542 under the flag of Spain in search of Cibola. There is little doubt he observed the golden poppy cascading across the foothills and meadows just off California's coast.

Cabrillo searched in vain for Cibola. It is no wonder, as Cibola, one of the legendary *seven cities of gold, was a myth.*

In the myth, the *seven cities of gold* grew very rich, mainly from gold and precious stones. This idea fueled many expeditions in search of the mythical cities during the following centuries.

Quivira and *Cibola* are two of the *Seven Cities of Gold* that exists only in a myth in a tale that originated about 1150 when the Moors conquered Merida, Spain.

The California poppy earned its position as the state's flower by establishing itself in most every county of the state. American Indians used the flower for medicinal purposes.
(Photo courtesy Martin Fletcher, California Gardens)

Adelbert von Chamisso, a naturalist on the Russian ship *Rurik*, first described the California poppy in 1820. He saw the flowers when the *Rurik* sailed into San Francisco.

California poppies were among the few plants still in flower in the month of August and Russian scientists marveled at their brilliant color. Chamisso named the genus in honor of Johann Friedrich Eschscholtz, the expedition's physician and Chamisso's close friend.

The California poppy grows over a wide range of territory and is not exclusive to California alone. It does grow in most every county in the state. The California poppy is technically a perennial but is often grown as an annual due to its ability to go from seed to flower in a matter of weeks. A single plant can flower profusely over a long period before setting seed and producing new flowering plants in the same season.

The poppy can be found in abundance in the Mojave Desert, southern Washington, Nevada, New Mexico and northwest Baja, California.

Indians used the California poppy for medicinal purposes. Francise Lloyd, in his *An Introduction to 81 California Wildflowers, Flowers of the Foothills*, wrote in 1973:

"The Indians ate the herbage, either boiling or roasting it and then putting it in water. It makes a drug like morphine and was used for headache and insomnia." Some say the foliage of the California poppy can be placed on an aching tooth and bring relief.

The Spanish call the flower *copa de oro*, or cup of gold.

Jeff Mayfield, a pioneer who arrived in California, wrote in 1850, "As we passed below the hills, the whole plain was covered with great patches of rose, yellow, scarlet, orange, and blue. The colors did not seem to mix to any great extent. Each kind of flower liked a certain kind of soil best, and some of the patches of one color were a mile or more across."

While the California poppy does not transplant well, its seeds can be sown in the fall or early spring directly into the soil. The poppies need full sun and a well-drained soil. The flowers become drought resistant once they become established on a site.

The blossom of the California poppy closes at night.

The California Poppy Reserve is located in the Antelope Valley on 1745 acres, where the California poppy grows unrestrained. The park does not water the poppies or provide any other maintenance.

Indians tell of another legend concerning the California poppy. Native Americans say it was the poppy that put the gold in the ground. The Indians say the flowers of the golden poppy were deposited in the earth after the plants shed their blooms.

Since becoming the state flower, the California poppy is now a protected plant. It is illegal to pick, destroy, or dig up a California poppy.

Chapter 20

Founder of San Francisco

William A. Richardson, founder of San Francisco.

William A. Richardson was born in London, England. He deserted an English whaler when it put into San Francisco in 1822. He was tall, fair-haired, blue-eyed and only 27 years old.

Richardson petitioned Spanish Governor Pablo Vicente Sola for permission to stay in California.

Permission was granted on one condition. Richardson must teach the neophytes at Mission Dolores how to construct small boats for use in the bay.

He taught carpentry, boatbuilding and navigation at the Mission. He also began building the first house of any substance in San Francisco. He planned to use the residence as a trading post.

He engaged in trading hides and tallow, and transported these supplies out of the Bay in small boats to the ocean-going ships that lay outside. At that time, none of the regular ocean-going liners came into the Bay.

He sold the pelts of otters to Boston traders for $40 to $60 each. Otters were plentiful in the bays and rivers of California.

During the Mexican period, he also bought and sold cattle hides. Some 50,000 to 80,000 hides were shipped from California to shoe factories in Massachusetts each year.

Cattle hides were an important medium of exchange in an economy still based on the barter system. Hides became known as "California's bank notes", and were worth about two dollars each.

Captain Richardson would later have the distinction of piloting the first deep-sea ship to enter San Francisco Bay, landing it in Sausalito.

At that early date, the only European communities were those located in the Presidio and the Mission. The European community consisted of Spanish soldiers and Spanish missionaries.

In 1823, Richardson converted to Catholicism. He became a naturalized citizen of Mexico, changed his name to Guillermo Antonio Richardson, and married a Mexican.

He took as his bride the daughter of Lieutenant Ygnacio Martinez, the Commandante of the Presidio.

Richardson acquired large tracts of land in Marin County, where he raised horses and cattle. He also owned two blocks now incorporated in the Presidio.

He built the first house in San Francisco. It was a large piece of canvas stretched on four posts and covered by an old ship sail. The house was located at what is now 823-827 Grant Avenue, near Clay Street. Two years later, he built a more substantial structure of adobe bricks.

Richardson had charge of several schooners belonging to Mission Dolores and one belonging to Mission Santa Clara.

One of his enterprises was operating a barge from Sausalito to San Francisco, carrying fresh water for the city.

When, in 1835, Governor Jose Figueroa made Yerba Buena (Now San Francisco) California's second port of entry, Richardson was offered the position of Port Captain.

In 1845, Richardson received a land grant covering a vast territory. He called this place *Albion* after his English homeland.

He built a sawmill on a river's estuary, powered by a tide-driven water wheel. The clever design allowed the mill to operate whenever the tide was changing. Immense waves destroyed the mill in 1853.

Richardson lost the land grant in 1854 because the U.S. Land Commission never recognized his ownership.

Chapter 21

Dam Collapse Kills 500

The St. Francis Dam was filled in the period 1926-28. It held enough water to supply Los Angeles for a full year.

(GRIM Society)

The St. Francis Dam contained enough water to quench the thirst of the one million, two hundred thousand people in Los Angeles for a year. The problem was, the dam leaked from the day it opened in 1926.

William Mulholland, chief engineer and head of Los Angeles Department of Water and Power.

(Google Images)

Folks in the farm towns downstream from the structure joked, "We'll see you later if the dam doesn't break."

Well, the dam did break. Its 12 billion gallons of water came crashing down San Francisquito Canyon taking 495 human lives with it. The true toll may be higher when undocumented farm workers are added to it.

At its peak, the wall of water was 78 feet high. It buried the town of Santa Paula. The flooding waters demolished 1,200 houses, washed out 10 bridges and knocked out power lines. Bodies washed ashore as far south as San Diego.

The St. Francis dam was located 50 miles north of Los Angeles. It was the project of William Mulholland, head of the Los Angeles Department of Water and Power.

Searchers look for bodies in the aftermath of the dam collapse. (Photo by Paul H. Rippens)

Mulholland built the dam as a backup water supply for Los Angeles. It was his insurance against a water shortage.

In hearings following the dam's collapsed, it became clear that Mulholland and other water officials, the day before the dam broke, had inspected water leaks in the dam.

On March 12, 1928, the dam keeper, Tony Harnischfeger, summoned Mulholland and his chief assistant Harvey Van Norman about muddy leaks coming from the dam.

Mulholland and Van Norman vouched for the dam's safety. Twelve hours later, Tony Harnischfeger and his 6-year-old son, Coder, were among the first to die in the ravaging waters.

The floodwater reached a crest of 40 feet by the time it traveled 18 miles downstream. It poured

133

over the tents of 150 men working for Edison, killing 84 of them.

One survivor, who struggled out of his car and clung to its hood, recalled, "There was a high fog, no stars, no moon, and all the lights were out in the valley. It was as dark as a closet."

The Los Angeles *Times* reported that California Highway Patrol officer Thornton Edwards was in Fillmore when the water slammed into the town. Edwards raced through the streets of Santa Paula, 42 miles from the dam, warning residents.

It was determined by an investigative committee that there were many problems with the design and placement of the dam.

The disaster's primary cause, however, was unstable geology. The dam's eastern edge sat on an ancient landslide that shifted and plowed into the structure like a bulldozer blade.

In his book, "Man-Made Disaster," Charles Outland explored the causes of the collapse further.

"One of the most dramatic pieces of visual evidence from the disaster is the reservoir water level chart, or Stevens Gauge. It drops precipitously at 11:57 a.m., a startling indication that the dam was down. But a gradual fall had begun hours beforehand. This would indicate a large outflow of water, but none of the survivors below the dam reported such a pre-flood."

Outland contends the Stevens Gauge was reporting a weakened abutment support, and that the enormous concrete structure was tilting. This caused the water level to drop against the upstream side of the dam.

A coroner's inquest laid the blame for the faulty dam on William Mulholland, which he publicly accepted. His career nosedived and never rose again.

In May 1927, about 10 months before St. Francis Dam collapsed, Los Angeles officials received phone warnings that sabotage might be imminent.

Owens Valley rancher Perry Sexton admitted that and other ranchers had dynamited the City's No Name Canyon siphon. The admission came in court after the St. Francis Dam failed. Los Angeles was taking their water and they wanted to stop it.

Water politics between the city of Los Angeles and the farmers of the Owens Valley were indeed strained. The farmers believed Los Angeles was stealing their water.

The collapse of the St. Francis Dam is considered the second-worst disaster in California history, the violent San Francisco earthquake of 1906 being worse.

Even though it was a disaster of epic proportions, it is little publicized or discussed today. One thing that surfaces in studies of the collapse is that it was a "Man-Made Disaster" due to faulty planning and use of faulty materials.

It was a disaster that should never have happened.

Chapter 22

Chinese Exclusion Act

In 1885, a Chinese head tax of fifty dollars was imposed in Canada to discourage immigration.

I t was an ugly law aimed at a single segment of the population.
The Chinese Exclusion Act was clearly racist and designed to restrict immigration of anyone from China.

Anti-Chinese sentiment began during the gold rush. People in California hated the Chinese for their industriousness and willingness to take on jobs that they themselves would not.

Cartoons and other propaganda against the Chinese immigrants reinforced the thinking of many in California, "The Chinese worked cheap and smelled bad," wrote Roger Daniels in his book "Asian America".

Racial tensions snapped in 1882. Congress passed the Chinese Exclusion Act of 1882. This act barred the immigration of Chinese to America for ten years. The act was extended for another ten years in 1892, and it was made permanent in 1904.

Chinese immigration to the U.S. continued, even in the face of the Chinese Exclusion Act. Authorities overlooked enforcement of the law. The Chinese became adept at using false names and identities, and coming to their so-called "relatives" already in the U.S. They became "paper" sons and daughters.

Americans had two complaints. One was that the Chinese were usurping jobs that Americans could fill because the Chinese were willing to work for smaller wages. Americans also claimed the Chinese were sending too much gold back to China.

The Chinese Exclusion Act of 1882 covered many facets of immigration.

The Act stipulated that the master of any vessel that knowingly brought a Chinese laborer to America would be guilty of a misdemeanor.

BOYCOTT

A General Boycott has been declared upon all CHINESE and JAPANESE Restaurants, Tailor Shops and Wash Houses. Also all persons employing them in any capacity.

All Friends and Sympathizers of Organized Labor will assist us in this fight against the lowering Asiatic standards of living and of morals.

AMERICA vs. ASIA
Progress vs. Retrogression
Are the considerations involved.

BY ORDER OF

Silver Bow Trades and Labor Assembly and Butte Miners' Union

A flyer posted calling for a boycott of Chinese and Japanese establishments.

Punishment would be a fine of not more than five hundred dollars for each Chinese laborer, with possible imprisonment for up to one year.

A Chinese mining camp in California in 1851.
(Wells Fargo History Room)

In 1849, at the start of the gold rush, there were only 54 Chinese in California. Gold fever swept through China just as it did the rest of the world. Ship captains distributed leaflets showing highly colored accounts of gold free for the picking in California. It proved to be more lucrative for the ship captains than it did for the workers.

The Chinese were, in fact, welcomed to California in 1849. In the fever of the gold rush, the Chinese filled positions as cooks, laundrymen and servants.

Chinese workers were in demand as laborers, carpenters and cooks. They were sought after for draining and tilling the rich tule lands. California Governor John McDougal referred to the Chinese laborer as "one of the most worthy of our newly adopted citizens."

A Chinese butcher and grocery shop in San Francisco during the gold rush. (Library of Congress)

The *Alta California* newspaper in San Francisco went so far as to say: "The China Boys will yet vote at the same polls, study at the same schools, and bow at the same altar as our countrymen."

The Chinese were welcome as long as the surface gold was plentiful for everyone.

The enormous number of miners seeking the gold on California's creeks soon depleted the surface gold. Disappointed miners turned their bitterness against other races in California, and the Frenchman, the Mexican, and the Chileno, were all targets

"California is for the Americans" became an anthem for gold seekers, but it was the Chinese that received the brunt of the criticism.

They dressed different, wore pigtails down the back of their necks, but worse, they were more efficient in gleaning the golden metal than were others.

Governor John Bigler
(Google Images)

The first law dealing with the issue was passed by the legislature in 1850. This was the Foreign Miners

License Law, which imposed a tax of twenty dollars a month on all foreign miners.

The law did not have its desired effect. San Francisco soon became overrun with penniless foreigners and their care became a problem. Legislators conceded the law was a failure and repealed it the following year.

As gold strikes became rare or non-existent, unemployed miners drifted back into San Francisco. The labor market was glutted, and Chinese workers, who worked harder and for less money, filled many of the jobs there.

In 1954, discovery of gold in Australia caused a financial panic in California. Prices of goods decreased, rents fell, and many business houses failed.

A prejudiced, anti-Chinese movement took hold in California. Some suggested that all Chinese be returned to China, but because the expense of such a movement would cost about seven million dollars, the idea died.

There was a rash of local ordinances passed to harass the Chinese. There was the famous "Pig Tail" ordinance, which required that all male prisoners have their hair cut within one-inch of their heads. The mayor vetoed this ordinance.

Labor groups detested the Chinese for taking their jobs during the depressed period of 1873. More and more they took matters into their own hands. Their antagonism led them to sack and burn Chinese laundries and other commercial establishments.

In Los Angeles, nineteen Chinese males were hanged and shot in one evening, and $40,000 worth of their goods stolen. California Governor John Bigler thought he could turn the Chinese situation into a political advantage.

In a message to the legislature, Bigler described the Chinese workers as "contract coolie labor." He said they were "avaricious, ignorant of moral obligations, incapable of being assimilated, and dangerous to public welfare."

He then proposed a renewal of the miner's tax, albeit in a milder form than its predecessor.

Bigler had a misguided notion of what a "coolie" actually was. The word itself comes from two words, *koo* meaning to rent, and *lee* meaning muscle. The coolies were thus those who rent out their muscles.

Of the four classes of workers in China, the coolie ranks with the third, being a higher class than merchants but below the scholars and farmers.

The Chinese Exclusion Act was repealed December 17, 1943, allowing the Chinese to legally immigrate to the U.S. again.

Chapter 23

Big 'Blowup' in Roseville

A giant fireball spews ammunition debris over the Roseville railroads in 1973.

(Roseville Carnegie Museum)

For years Mayor George Buljan and Police Chief James Hall knew their city was living in danger.

145

They knew the possibility existed that one of the munitions trains going through Roseville, California might blow up some day.

One did!

At 8:07 a.m., an explosion rocked a 100-mile area. Firemen backed out of the raging fire as soon as they learned it was a powder keg of bombs and bomb fragments lying all over the place.

Blasts were so loud that law enforcement officers covered their ears to prevent damage.

(Roseville Historical Society)

The explosions lasted for five hours, ripping through the bomb-laden freight train like a slow-moving string of giant firecrackers. The explosions leveled the little town of Antelope, sitting next to the railroad tracks.

Fifty-two people were taken to area hospitals but no deaths occurred.

Newsmen and highway patrolman crouch behind a patrol car during the explosion. (Roseville Historical Society)

Three to five thousand residents were evacuated from their homes within a three-mile radius of the explosion. The evacuation area was later reduced to one mile. Residents returned to their homes at 8:30 p.m., facing the prospect of no gas or electricity.

An emergency worker protects his ear during explosion.
(Roseville Historical Society)

Hundreds of trains loaded with munitions made the trip through Roseville during World War II and during the wars in Korea and Vietnam. The train arrived at the Roseville Yard entrance at 0605 and was staged in the westward department yard by 0630.

Since the train was too long for the yard, the forward cars (the ones that exploded) were placed on a track well separated from the remaining three cars, which were loaded with more than 1,000 bombs. These three cars were saved with only minor damage. The bombs were securely blocked and braced and in perfect condition.

Southern Pacific Railroad officials reported that a chain of explosions began at 7:52 a.m., soon after an employee spotted smoke in one of the cars of the 103-unit train.

The train contained 21 Department of Defense freight cars, each carrying 330 unfused Mark 81 bombs weighing 250 pounds each. The train carried two million pounds of explosives.

One resident, thrown from his bed by the explosion, ran out to see what was happening. A giant mushroom cloud and another smaller explosion confronted him. He got his wife and four children to a neighbor who drove them to a relative's home.

Nearby McClellan Air Force Base dispatched doctors and medical corpsmen to assist. Additional military help came from the Presidio in San Francisco and Alameda Naval Air Station and from Hamilton Air Force Base.

Law enforcement officers set up a command center three-fourths mile from the blast center. A hail of shrapnel rained down on them, causing them to move their command base back to four miles away from the blast.

Two hundred National Guard troops of the 1st Battalion, 184th Infantry in Sacramento were activated to prevent looting and to man roadblocks.

Some witnesses reported seeing a "red-hot wheel" on a railcar. Rail officials determined that a faulty brake shoe caused the fire, setting off the propane tank explosions on two non-military propane gas cars.

The Sacramento *Bee* reported:

> *The explosions rippled through hundreds of other freight cars in the vast yard. And outside the yard itself, thousands of area residents were shaken into wakefulness.*

Sheriff's deputies and highway patrol officers stopped several drivers leaving the blast area with "souvenir bombs" in the trunks of their cars.

The bombs were so large that some couldn't close the trunk lids. One officer said the driver of a Volkswagen bug had a 250-pound munitions bomb stuffed into its front-facing trunk.

As a direct result of the Roseville explosion, spark shields above railcar wheels and non-sparking brake shoes are required.

In 1974, Congress passed the Transportation Safety Act, which brought together numerous regulations by various agencies into one publication. Also, the law placed responsibility for shipping hazardous materials on everyone, be it the shipper, carrier or receiver.

Munitions trains still move through Roseville.

Chapter 24

Crazy Stoddard's
Lost Lake of Gold

(It is with the author's permission and our pleasure that we reprint this article that originally ran in "The Feather River Territorial", Fall-Winter issue, 1960-61. James W. Lenhoff published the 'Territorial')

By James Lenhoff

It was shortly after dawn in the early fall of 1849 that a small wagon train rolled from its campsite near what is today Reno, Nevada. The party was bound for Marysville and the surrounding gold fields.

The crisp morning air brought with it warnings of an early winter. Occasional snow flurries already capped the highest peaks of the Sierra with a crown of white. Because of this, the group decided to head northwest until they reached a trail leading down to the Sacramento Valley.

The detour might take a few days longer, but the travelers preferred the loss of time to the horrors of another Donner tragedy with its starvation, murder and cannibalism.

153

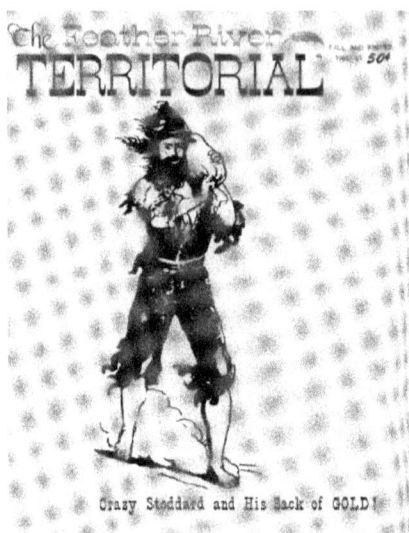

Crazy Stoddard's story was publishing in the Feather River Territorial.

(Courtesy James Lenhoff)

The captain of the train called for two volunteers to hunt for game along the ridge they would skirt ahead. A fellow by the name of Thomas Stoddard stepped forward.

He was a young, fair-haired Englishman who had been in the British Navy and had taught briefly back in Pennsylvania before getting "gold fever" and heading west. The name of the other man is not known.

The two men walked a couple of miles when they came across the fresh tracks of a grizzly bear. If they could bag this animal there would be plenty of steaks for everyone in the train. They decided to track the bear.

154

They had a strong pack mule with them and could easily carry back the meat. They spotted the bear in a thicket, and with two well-placed shots, Stoddard brought the beast down. They skinned and quartered the bear and prepared to go back to the wagon train.

They spotted a grizzly.

During their intense tracking efforts, they forgot to keep tabs on the direction they took after the bear. The men were lost.

To make matters worse, an icy squall enveloped them, laying a thick carpet of snow over any tracks they might have used to retrace their steps. Realizing they were at least temporarily lost, Stoddard and his companion decided to camp for the night.

Several days later, the two men were still roaming the mountainsides, seeking a glimpse of Long Valley where the wagon train was headed. As they peered at the dark canyons and white peaks of the great Sierra, they did notice one peculiar characteristic. There was an abundance of lakes.

At one point, they spied a small party of Indians coming behind them. Attempts to communicate with them proved futile as the red men disappeared into the forest when approached.

As evening approached, Stoddard and his companion led their mule up to a large granite shelf protruding from the base of a large bluff. As his companion made a rock barrier to ward off the wind as well as a possible Indian attack, Stoddard looked over the edge of the cliff. Two hundred feet below was a beautiful lake.

Indians shot arrows at the two men, killing Stoddard's companion.

He took a couple of canvas bags to fetch some water. He kneeled at the small stream feeding the lake to take a drink.

Stoddard immediately drew back in amazement. The creek appeared to be lined with thousands of gold pebbles. He probed the creek bottom, scooping up a handful of the shiny pellets.

He smashed one with a heavy rock and it flattened out like it was pure gold. Stoddard knew there was no doubt that he had found gold.

He shouted to his partner to come see what he had found. While his partner scrambled down the mountainside, Stoddard filled a bag with nuggets.

While they were rejoicing over their windfall, they were sobered by the death cry of their mule. From above, several Indians began firing a volley of arrows at them. As Stoddard leaped for a boulder to screen himself from the warriors, one of the arrows tore into the flesh of his leg.

His partner was less fortunate. Two arrows lodged hard into his back and he fell face down in the creek, his hands clutching at the bed of nuggets he would never spend.

Stoddard fired at the Indians. He saw one of them pitch back onto the shelf and the Indians fled, taking the fallen body with them.

His partner and his mule both dead, Stoddard was now alone, surrounded by an incredible fortune in gold. Stoddard settled down for the night to ponder his situation.

The next morning, he climbed to the top of the ridge and sighted what he described as the highest buttes he had ever seen. From there, he figured he could get his bearings.

Stoddard then placed 400 ounces of gold (thirty-four pounds) in a sling and strapped it to his back. He dumped the rest into the lake.

Tattered and hungry, he stumbled out of the wilderness and into a little mining camp on the Yuba River, a few miles above Downieville. A couple of miners took Stoddard to their cabin, fed him some hot soup and wrapped him in their heavy coats. They allowed him to soak his feet in a gold pan filled with warm water.

Stoddard told the men about his harrowing adventure and the fabulous lake filled with gold. The miners pretended to listen, but agreed that the poor man was hallucinating.

When Stoddard dumped the cache of nuggets on the table in front of them, they formed a different opinion. The miners agreed it was too late in the season to return to the mountains. A harsh winter would spell certain death.

Snow squalls were already spilling their flakes of snow against the cabin door. The lake would have to keep its hoard of nuggets until spring.

Stoddard stayed around Downieville to get back his strength. When he felt well, he went down the Yuba River in search of any members of his wagon train party.

To his surprise, he found the story of his lake of gold had preceded him. In camp after camp, he could hear the snickers and sarcastic remarks such as: *There goes Crazy Stoddard. Whoever heard of a lake filled with pure gold?*

In Marysville, Stoddard tried to interest the proprietor of the Western Hotel into outfitting an expedition. The man listened attentively as Stoddard drew a map giving the general direction of the lake.

A Negro waiter fussed about their table until he was ordered to go someplace else. The proprietor declined Stoddard's suggestion, choosing to attend his thriving hotel business.

Stoddard then boarded a steamer for San Francisco, where he learned his wagon party had made it to California but had scattered to the rich diggings around Nevada City.

He returned again to Marysville where he bought a horse and headed for Nevada City. Everywhere he went, people hounded him to organize an expedition. His tale of the lake of gold had spread everywhere.

Stoddard rode into Nevada City (then Deer Creek Dry Diggins) and saw shacks and tents crowding each other on the flats. He met George E. Britten a miner and after considerable talk, showed him his gold nuggets.

Britten was a man of action. He contacted twenty-five men who could be counted on to keep their mouths shut, and scheduled a party to leave within two weeks.

When the time came, they stole away by night and met at a rendezvous on the southern Yuba River. They brought along a score of pack mules to haul their golden hoard.

The party began its ascent up the North San Juan Ridge the next morning. They traveled twelve miles the first day, and stopped at a dilapidated hostelry in Deerville.

At the inn, the proprietor said, "I thought you was another party of them Gold Lakers. Been lots of 'em through now that the trail is open. Makes for real good business. Too bad they can't locate that Stoddard feller who discovered..."

The proprietor then recognized Stoddard. He sent a rider alerting every mining camp in the area that Stoddard was heading for his golden lake. The proprietor of the inn accomplished his goal.

He made a small fortune selling provisions at exorbitant prices to the throngs that came to see Stoddard's lake. Men abandoned good-paying jobs to join the throng. The population had gone berserk with a new epidemic of gold fever.

Miners combed the mountains south of Quincy, west of Donner Lake, north of Downieville and east of Oroville in that summer of 1850.

Stoddard's party managed to elude the followers, but his troubles began when he couldn't lead them directly to his lake. The land looked different to him without its carpet of snow.

To confuse matters more, rockslides had been added to the old ones. Day after day, they ascended one ridge after another hoping to find a familiar landmark.

The men in the party grew testy and little by little, the name "Crazy Stoddard" came into use again as the men plodded on.

It was suggested that the party move to the Reno area where Stoddard first started in search of the grizzly bear. Perhaps he could retrace his steps from that direction.

The miners struggled down the Yuba Pass. They finally landed in a plush green valley which took them all by surprise. It stretched into a huge triangular shape, rimmed by towering peaks that were lost above the clouds.

Here was soil rich enough for a thousand farms, but these were men blinded by their quest for gold. Valley.

Still Stoddard couldn't find the direction to his lake of gold. Confusion gave way to panic when threats were cast his way. The party moved on, finally fumbling its way into a small valley late one afternoon.

The men insisted on camping, eating in silence a meal of dry biscuits and jerky. Finally, one of the miners stood.

> *Well, Stoddard, this is your last chance. If you don't find the lake by tomorrow sundown we are going to hang you by your blasted neck. Right boys?*

When the men rolled into their blankets, George Britten, the leader of the miners, nudged Stoddard.

> *Slip out of that sack and saddle old Jack. He's the best mule of the lot. Get on him and get the hell out of here.*

"How about you?" Stoddard asked.

> *I'll be alright. It's you they're mad at not me. Someday we'll get together and find that lake.*

Stoddard walked the mule out of camp, mounted and sped away from the valley that still bears the name of *Last Chance Valley*.

Records indicate that Stoddard reached Downieville and lived there for several years as a respected citizen. He and his wife spent the summers searching for his lake of gold but never found it.

At least two others had better luck. The Negro waiter in the Marysville hotel quit his job that spring and returned a few weeks later to show the hotel owner a bulging sack of nuggets. He claimed to have scooped them up from the Golden Lake. He left on a steamer the next day for Peru, where he lived in retirement for the rest of his life.

A year later, in 1851, a Canadian trapper named Deloreaux rode wild-eyed into Downieville. His leather satchels were bulging with gold nuggets. He claimed to have discovered Stoddard's Golden Lake.

Chapter 25

The Lost Cement Mines

If history records the story correctly, it was three German brothers escaping from Indians that discovered the Lost Cement Mines.

The brothers, according to Mark Twain who recounts the tale in his book, "Roughing It", found a ledge "as wide as a curbstone", of reddish cement, two-thirds of it pure gold.

The tale has persisted down through history, adopting a few twists and turns of its own, but is still believed to be basically true.

No less a historian than the late Walter Chalfant, editor of the Inyo Register, wrote about the mystical mine.

According to Chalfant's version, the Germans reached the Sierra at the head of Owens River while fleeing Indians. There, they found a ledge of reddish cement protruding that contained rich gold.

The men took out about twenty-five pounds of the ore, covered up the ledge and then resumed their journey.

Two of the three brothers perished in the mountains. The third made his way through to a west-side mining camp, physically and mentally deranged.

The few fragments of ore he still retained created a stir in the camp. The German refused to return to the site where he found the ore, but he did give Gid Whiteman a description and a crude map of the region.

Mammoth Mountain can be seen from atop this cement spur that some believe is the possible site of the Lost Cement Mine.

Other similar, but slightly different versions of the Lost Cement Mines have appeared. J.W.A. Wright, a *San Francisco Post* writer, wrote about the mine being found in 1879.

In this version, the mine was found by two California-bound men who left the wagon train and traveled to the head of the Owens River in the Sierra.

They described their travel through "the burnt country". They sat down to rest near a spring or stream.

Here, they observed a curious-looking rock and began pounding and crushing it. They saw in it a quantity of what appeared to be gold. One man insisted it was gold, the other one laughed at him.

The believer took about ten pounds of the ore with him. They crossed the rough Sierra, making their way to the San Joaquin River.

The man carrying the ore became consumptive and went to San Francisco for treatment.

Before he could return to the treasure, he became so ill that he had to abandon the idea.

He had no money with which to pay his physician, a Dr. Randall. He gave the doctor his remaining ore and a rough map of the country, and some minute details.

An outcrop above the discovery site of the Lost Cement Mine.

Randall traveled to old Monoville in 1861, intent on finding the Lost Cement Mines. He hired some men to accompany him to what was called Pumice Flat, about eight miles north of Mammoth Canyon. He put a claim on 160 acres.

The physician returned the following year and employed Gid Whiteman to head a prospecting crew. With the old prospector's map, Whiteman scoured the entire 160-acres. They found reddish lava or cement. Specimens shown by Randall were rich in gold.

Excitement soared and prospectors poured out of Aurora and Monoville. Never was there a greater furor over a mining find. From 1862 to 1879, not a year passed but from one to twenty parties spent part of the summer searching for the treasure.

Mark Twain
(Google Images)

Even Gid Whiteman, head of Randall's prospecting party, commented about the Mark Twain account: "The real facts of the original find were not so well-known then as now. Friend Mark was giving us humor rather than history."

A Los Angeles geologist, Christer Loftenius says the Lost Cement Mine contains nothing more than a form of fool's gold. Loftenius decided to try and locate the missing mine.

He and his colleagues used the same information written about by Mark Twain and J.W.A. Wright to seek the location of the mine.

Previous searches focused on the area north of Mammoth Lakes at the head of the Owens River. The Owens River flows southeast along the Long Valley Caldera—a 32-kilometer-long depression that formed 760,000 years ago when a volcano erupted.

Noting that Wright's description of visibility to the southeast for up to a kilometer, Loftenius limited his search to the only area that fit this description, which was the caldera's rim, as opposed to regions inside the caldera.

Loftenius next set out to determine if a gold deposit located north of the mountain would be geologically feasible. Areas north of Mammoth Mountain were never known to harbor any sources of gold.

He located a ridge of bedrock, called the cement spur that most likely could support the formation and discovery of gold. He and his colleagues found rocks that matched those described in the Lost Cement Mine accounts.

The rocks turned out to be marble. Inside cracks of the red marble, the researchers found the "gold" was actually flakes of white mica that had been stained yellow by iron oxide, forming a type of "fool's gold".

Loftenius is rather certain that the cement spur was the same one described by Twain and Wright. He wonders if the legend was perpetuated as a ruse to bring in investors to finance development of mining prospects north of Mammoth.

Chapter 26

The Sea Otter Hunters

A privateer called the *Otter* dropped anchor at Monterey in 1796. It was the first American vessel to visit California, not yet a part of the United States.

Ebenezer Dorr, who carried a passport signed by President George Washington and countersigned by the Spanish consul at Charleston, South Carolina, commanded the *Otter*.

The ship arrived at Monterey after sailing across the Pacific from Australia. The purpose of the visit was to land some English stowaways who got on board in Australia. The *Otter* lacked sufficient accommodations for them.

Captain Dorr was refused permission to discharge the English stowaways. Dorr then clandestinely put the unwelcome Englishmen ashore at gunpoint.

This angered Governor Diego de Borica who felt his Spanish hospitality had been repaid with crude conduct. His attitude toward the Englishmen changed, however, when he learned that they were artisans.

He put them to work as carpenters and blacksmiths. The Englishmen proved to be such good workers and so well behaved that Governor

Borica regretted it when Royal orders came to send them to San Blas.

The *Otter* was the first of many United States ships to begin working the California coast for sea otter skins.

Following the *Otter's* contact with the area, American interest in California escalated. Despite Spanish objections, Yankee skippers continued to work the California coast.

A procession of sea otter hunters followed. In 1799, Captain James Rowan anchored his ship, *Eliza* at Yerba Buena (San Francisco). In 1800, the *Betsy*, under Captain Charles Winship, dropped anchor. Captain Joseph O'Cain, a notorious otter hunter, sailed into San Quentin in 1804, for repairs.

Some Americans were jailed for violating Mexican laws in regard to taking sea otters. The price of sea otter pelts gave them good reason for taking their chances.

A single sea otter pelt could bring from $40 to $140 at Canton, China.

The Russians soon joined the Americans in pursuit of the abundant sea otter. The Kashaya Indians assembled to watch the spectacle as the Russians anchored in the cove beneath their quiet bluff top settlement.

The Indians continued to watch as the twenty-five Russians and eight Alaskans came ashore, set up a temporary camp. In wonderment, they watched as the foreigners began building houses and a sturdy stockade (Fort Ross).

This watercolor shows Fort Ross as seen by artist Il'ia Voznesenky, 1841.

The Russians had come to hunt sea otter, but also to grow wheat and other crops for the Russian settlements in Alaska. Their intent was to also open trade with Spanish California.

Less talked about, was their intent on continuing their eastward expansion, a process that began in the time of Ivan the Terrible, Russia's first Tsar.

The Russian presence in the North Pacific induced Spain to occupy Alta California in 1769. By 1812, San Francisco Bay still marked the limit of Spanish settlement.

The British, too, were anxious to have California. One promoter of British presence in California was Alexander Forbes, a merchant. He talked of the possibility of British investors taking California in recompense for the $50 million debt owed to them by Mexico.

Some British newspapers picked up the idea and promoted it as a good plan to follow.

Index

Alameda Naval Air Station, 149

Albion, 129

Alcatraz, 7, 55, 56, 58, 59, 60, 106

Alta California, 25, 26, 31, 33, 142, 171

Alvarado, Juan Batista, 117

American River Conservancy, 83

An Introduction to California Wildflowers, 81, 125

Anza-Borrego Desert, 87

Apache Rebellions, 107

Ayala, Juan Manuel, 55

Baja, California, 125

Bank of America, 68, 79

Bank of Italy, 75, 77, 78, 79

Banks, Homer, 66, 77

Battle of La Mesa, 32

Bauer, Captain George William, 39, 40

Beebe, William, 53

Big Foot, 110

Bigler, Governor John, 144

Birmingham, 41, 42

Borica, Governor Diego, 169, 170

Boyd, Ed, 18, 20

Bridgeport, 74

British Royal Navy, 44

Britten, George E., 159, 161

Brother Jonathan, 120

Broughton, Jack, 96, 97, 98, 99

Buljan, Mayor George, 145

Bureau of Land Management, 17, 19, 82, 84

Cabrillo, Juan Rodriguez, 25, 123

California, 8, 12, 13, 17, 18, 22, 24, 25, 26, 27, 28, 29, 30, 31, 33, 35, 36, 37, 38, 39, 45, 47, 60, 63, 64, 68, 69, 72, 73, 74, 78, 79, 82, 85, 86, 89, 95, 97, 98, 109, 115, 116, 117, 123, 124, 125, 126, 127, 128, 129,

134, 135, 138, 140,
142, 143, 144, 146,
159,164, 169, 170,
171, 180
California
   Department of
   Public Works., 22
California Poppy
   Reserve, 126
California State Floral
   Society, 123
Calochortus, 123
Camby, General
   Edward, 103
Capone, Al, 59, 60
Captain Jack, 101,
   102, 103, 104, 105,
   106, 107, 108
Carson Valley, 73
Carson, Mrs.
   Thankful A., 110,
   112, 113
Carson, Mrs.
   Tjhankful A., 73,
   109, 110, 111
Casa Romantica, 67,
   68
Castaic, 14
Castillo, Edward, 26,
   27
Chalfant, Walter, 163
Chamisso, Adelbert,
   124

Chicano, 33
Chinese Exclusion
   Act, 9, 137, 138, 144
Cibola, 123, 124
Claremont Institute,
   36
Colorado, 18, 22, 36
Colorado River, 18, 22
Cornelius, W.S., 45,
   46, 47, 48
Cosumnes River, 81,
   82, 83, 84, 85, 86
Curly-Headed Doctor,
   106
Daniels, Roger, 138
Deerville, 159
del Valle, Antonio,
   117
Department of
   Defense, 149
Department of
   Justice, 57
Desert Sun, 88
Dogtown Territorial
   Quarterly, 109
Donner Lake, 160
Donner Pass, 70
Dorr, Ebenezer, 169
Downieville, 157, 158,
   160, 161, 162
Dragon Rocks, 119
Drake, Francis, 25
Ducks Unlimited, 84

El Camino hotel, 50
Ely, Eugene Burton, 41
Emeryville Shell Mound, 96
Eschscholtz, Friedrich, 125
Eschscholzia californica, 123
Esmeralda County, 73
Faaborg, John, 99
Figueroa, Governor Jose, 129
Fletcher, Ed, 18, 20, 22, 124
Flores, General Jose Maria, 31, 32, 33
Foreign Miners License Law, 143
Fort Ross, 170, 171
Fremont, Lt.-Col John C., 32, 33
Ghost Mountain, 87, 89, 91, 92
Giannini, Amadeo Peter, 75, 76, 77, 78, 79
Gorge, 82, 83
Gray, L.F. "Newt", 21, 22
Great Britain, 36
Great Depression, 57
Gulf of Mexico, 33

Hall, Police Chief James, 145
Hamilton Air Force Base, 149
Hanson, Ole, 7, 61, 62, 63, 64, 65, 66, 67, 68
Holtville, 20, 23, 24
Honey Lake Valley, 70, 71, 73
Hooker Jim, 106
Humboldt Bay, 122
Imperial Sand Hills, 18
Island of the Pelicans, 55
Johnston, James A., 59, 60
Kearny, Stephen Watts, 31, 33
King, Charles, 7, 49, 50, 51, 52, 53
Klamaths, 101, 102, 107
Lassen County, 70
Last Chance Valley, 161
Lenhoff, James, 153, 154
Leonard, John, 111
Lewis, Samuel Mary Ann, 109
Little Big Horn, 107
Little Dry Creek, 109

Live Oak Canyon, 117
Lloyd, Francise, 125
Loftenius, Christer, 166, 167
Long Valley Caldera, 166
Lopez, Jose Francisco, 36, 116, 117
Los Angeles County, 118
Los Angeles Department of Water and Power, 132
Los Angeles Examiner, 18
Los Angeles *Herald Examiner*, 64
Los Angeles *Times*, 134
Los Angeles Tribune, 89
Lost Cement Mines, 9, 163, 164, 165
Mad River, 122
Maidu, 47
Mammoth Canyon, 165
Mammoth Mountain, 164, 167
Marin County, 129

Marysville, 30, 45, 153, 158, 159, 162
Massachusetts, 128
Mayfield, Jeff, 125
McClellan Air Force Base, 149
McDougal, Governor John, 140
Mexican, 31, 32, 33, 34, 36, 50, 78, 116, 128, 129, 142, 170
Mexico, 30, 33, 34, 35, 36, 88, 118, 128, 171
Model A Ford, 118
Model T Ford, 20
Modoc War, 102, 107
Modocs, 101, 102, 103, 104, 105, 107, 108
Mojave Desert, 125
Mokelumne River, 82
Mono County, 74
Monoville, 165, 166
Monterey, 49, 50, 51, 169
Monterey Bay, 49, 50
Mt. Lassen, 47, 48
Mulholland, William, 132, 133, 135
Naciemiento River., 53
Nataqua, 72

National Guard of California, 38
Native Americans, 26, 27, 96, 97, 99, 126
Nature Conservancy, 83
Naval Militia Act, 39
Naval Militia Corps, 39
Nevada, 36, 69, 71, 72, 73, 74, 82, 125, 153, 159
New Mexico, 35, 36, 125
Newhall, 118
Nez Perce, 107
Norman, Harvey Van, 89, 133
North Beach, 76
O'Cain, Joseph, 170
Oceanside Blade, 89
Okalahoma, 108
Old Ridge Route, 8, 11, 12, 13, 14, 15
Orange County Board of Supervisors, 68
Oregon, 38, 101, 103, 107
Oroville, 109, 160
Outland, Charles, 134
Owens River, 163, 164, 166
Owens Valley, 135

Panama Canal, 19
Pennsylvania, 42, 43, 44, 154
Philadelphia Mint, 117
Phoenix, 18
Phoenix, Arizona, 18
Pico, Andres, 33
Pierce, E.H., 72, 73
Placerita Canyon, 115, 116, 117, 118
Plumas County, 69, 71, 72, 73
Point St. George, 119
Polk, President James K., 34, 35, 36
Potter Hotel, 64
Pumice Flat, 165
Quincy, 160
Richardson, William A., 127, 128, 129, 130
Riddle, Winema "Toby", 107
Rio Grande, 34
Romneya coulteri, 123
Roop, Isaac, 69, 70, 71, 72, 73, 74
Rowan, James, 170
Rurik, 124
Sacramento *Bee*, 150
Sacramento Valley, 45, 46, 97, 153

Sagebrush War, 72
Salinas River, 49, 53
Salinas Valley, 49, 50, 51, 52, 53
San Antonio River, 53
San Clemente, 61, 65, 66, 68
San Diego, 18, 19, 20, 31, 37, 64, 65, 93, 132
San Fernando Mission, 118
San Francisco, 8, 42, 43, 75, 76, 77, 96, 98, 99, 124, 127, 128, 129, 135, 141, 142, 143, 149, 159, 164, 165, 170, 171
San Francisquito Canyon, 132
San Gabriel Fault Zone, 118
San Gabriel River, 31
San Joaquin Valley, 11
San Lorenzo Rancho, 50
Santa Anna, Antonio Lopez, 36
Santa Barbara, 64
Santa Paula, 77, 132, 134
Sasquach, 47

Sausalito, 128, 129
Scatena, 76
Schweichler, Margaret, 90
Seattle, 63, 64
Serra, Junipero, 27
Sierra Nevada, 73
Soberanes, Feliciana, 50
Sola, Governor Pablo Vicente, 127
Soledad, 51
Sonoma State University, 26
South, Marshal, 87, 89, 90, 91, 92, 93, 169
Southern Pacific Milling Company, 52
Southern Pacific Railroad, 51, 149
Spanish Village by the Sea, 64
Spreckels Sugar Company, 52
St. Francis Dam, 131, 135
St. George Reef Light, 121, 122
Starbuck, George, 118
Steinbeck, J. E., 51

Stockton, Captain Robert F., 31, 33
Stoddard, Thomas, 9, 153, 154, 155, 156, 157, 158, 159, 160, 161, 162
Straits of Juan de Fuca, 40
Susanville, 70, 71, 73
Sutter's Mill, 27
Taylor, General Zachary, 34
Texas, 33, 34, 36
The Giant Spirit Bear, 47
The Rustler, 53
The Treaty of Guadalupe-Hidalgo, 35
Twain, Mark, 163, 166, 167
Twenty-Nine Palms, 68
U.S. Department of the Navy, 39
Utah, 36, 71, 95, 96

Vancouver, George, 119
Vanderhurst, William, 52
Vernon, 32
Warder, Michael, 36
Washington, 64, 106, 125, 169
Washoe County, 73
Wheaton, Lt. Col. Frank, 103, 104, 105, 106
White Medicine Deer, 47
Whiteman, Gid, 164, 166
Willows, 45
Winship, Charles, 170
Wright, J.W.A., 164, 166, 167
Wyoming, 36
Yankee Jim, 47
Yaquitepec, 88, 91
Yerba Buena, 129, 170
Yuba River, 30, 157, 158, 159
Yuma, 18, 22, 23, 24

About the Author

Alton Pryor

Alton Pryor has been a writer for magazines, newspapers, and wire services for more than fifty years. He worked for United Press International in their Sacramento Bureau, handling both printed press and radio news.

He then moved to Salinas, where he worked for the Salinas Californian daily newspaper for five years as editor of Western Ranch and Home, a weekend supplement.

In 1963, he joined California Farmer magazine where he worked as a field editor for 27 years. When that magazine sold, the new owners forced him into temporary retirement. He gained an intense interest in California and Western history after selling a number of short 500-word articles on Southern California history.

In his research of these stories, he found other historical stories that interested him but did not fit the publication for which he was then writing. He began collecting facts and ideas, storing them on his computer and finally turned them into his first book, "Little Known Tales in California History."

Alton Pryor is now the author of 30-plus books. He is a graduate of California State Polytechnic University, San Luis Obispo, where he earned a Bachelor of Science degree in journalism.